Behavior and Training of Dogs and Puppies

Louis L. Vine, D.V.M.

ARCO PUBLISHING, INC.
219 PARK AVENUE SOUTH, NEW YORK, N.Y. 10003

Portions of this book were originally published in
Your Dog: His Health and Happiness,
copyright © 1971 by Louis L. Vine.

Second Printing, 1979

Published 1977 by Arco Publishing , Inc.
219 Park Avenue South, New York, N.Y. 10003

Library of Congress Cataloging in Publication Data

Vine, Louis L
  Behavior and training of dogs and puppies.

  Includes index.
  SUMMARY: A guide for understanding, training, and
caring for dogs. Includes information on abnormal
behavior and how it can be corrected.
  1. Dogs—Behavior. 2. Dogs—Training. [1. Dogs]
I. Title.

SF433.V55   636.7′08′8   77-1387
ISBN 0-668-04156-0 (Library Edition)
ISBN 0-668-04162-5 (Paper Edition)

Printed in the United States of America

There is no such thing as a puppy that is not capable of being taught or trained.

CONTENTS

INTRODUCTION

There is a boundless amount of erroneous and misleading "expert" advice on canine behavior available from dog-less relatives, friends, and neighbors, and from self-styled "dog trainers." Fortunately, this can be offset by the very excellent advice now available because of the combined efforts of dog psychologists, veterinarians, and obedience trainers in dealing with behavior problems.

It is important to state at the outset that not all behavior problems stem from bad management or a poor owner-pet relationship. Neuroses can be caused by heredity, faulty metabolism, brain injury, or other internal physical abnormalities. So a misbehaving or hard-to-teach pet should by all means be checked by a veterinarian.

In all studies of dog behavior problems the basic ingredient to be dealt with is the owner-pet relationship. It must be understood that all members of the family come under the term "owner," and all of the family's behaviors and attitudes can make a good pet or an incorrigible dog.

Many dog owners are innocent victims of a dominating pet that assumes control of things. The owners just don't have enough knowledge to cope with their clever but misguided animals. When the dog assumes dominance, he resorts to all kinds of abnormal behavior such as growling, mounting legs, whining relentlessly when he wants attention, and urinating on household effects. Once he is allowed to assume leadership, it is a difficult role to break, so he shouldn't be given the chance.

Researchers all agree that the most important and impressionable time in a dog's life is the socialization period—between eight and 12 weeks of age. This is the time when the puppy needs human companionship, love, and the training that makes for a happy and contented dog. An "unhappy childhood" can well result in a misbehaving dog that might have to be destroyed.

Obedience training is the key to a good owner-dog relationship. But in the training program you must immediately establish yourself as the BOSS. Even just by teaching the dog to respond to commands such as "come," "sit," and "stay" will help you establish yourself as leader. You have to be more stubborn than your dog. You have to show him that your will is stronger than his. YOU are HIS leader.

In all lessons to correct misbehavior, it is important that the dog owner be personally involved in the training. In the training program, the owner should follow the professional advice of a dog psychologist, veterinarian, or obedience trainer, and both dog and owner will benefit—a stronger bond of admiration, love, and respect will evolve.

1 PERSONALITY AND INTELLIGENCE

PERSONALITY

Because of behavior patterns the origin of the domestic dog is still being debated. Most scientists believe that today's dog is a descendant of the true northern wolf, although some experts in the field, and especially Lorenz, foremost authority on animal behavior, believe that the Asiatic jackal is the ancestor of certain of our breeds.

Regardless of origin, the ancestor of the dog was a pack hunter and strictly monogamous. Even today there's great chivalry in male dogs toward bitches and puppies. It is rare indeed for a male dog to pick a fight with a female dog. He normally will let her get away with a lot of female temperament, including being attacked by her, although he will defend himself from destruction.

Just as with the human species, and even though you may find yourself swearing that they are identical, no two dogs are exactly alike, be it in features and traits, temperament, personality, or intelligence—and certainly in behavior. In a group of dogs we will often see almost every personality type and temperament: the leader, the follower, the brave one, the coward, the sly one, the dumb one, the friendly one, the timid one, and of course always the bully. And even though you may often have heard, from numerous "authorities," that mutts are smarter than pedigreed dogs, and other sweeping generalizations such as that poodles are exceptionally smart, retrievers are very friendly, and German shepherds are suspicious of people and not to be trusted, none of these statements is true. Every degree of intelligence and every personality type can be found in every breed and mixture.

9

As the dog's personality is the sum total of his physical, mental, emotional, and social characteristics, and of the organized pattern of his behavioral characteristics, experience and training in early puppyhood determine the animal's personality and temperament. Dogs are born with certain instincts, and the training of these instincts, and the surrounding environment, mold their temperaments and personalities. Proper training and a favorable environment produce a dog of even temperament with a pleasant personality.

INTELLIGENCE: ROTE OR REASON?

Dogs seem to be getting keener of mind, and in fact many are progressing faster than humans. They're more aware of us —know us better than we know them. Their lives are centered on us. We are their reason for being—to love us, comfort us, serve us, help us in any way. I firmly believe that dogs understand more than people give them credit for, that they understand what we're saying—not every word and detail, but they get the gist, the essential meaning, of our conversation.

There is growing controversy between psychologists and dog owners on whether remarkable performances of dogs are the result of training or indicate reasoning power and judgment. I am not a psychologist, and I am prejudiced. There is much evidence that convinces me that many dogs have a high degree of intelligence. Psychologists contend that as dog training mostly involves repetition, dogs learn only by conditioned reflexes. But anyone who has ever trained a dog has surely found that the time comes when he really has to exert himself mentally to stay one step ahead of his canine pupil; the dog shows reasoning power to either avoid the work at hand or, if he cares to, to become an obedience champion. I have seen many dogs show judgment in thoughtfully appraising certain situations and then carefully take the right action. And certainly the judgment exercised by some Seeing Eye dogs shows intelligence far beyond conditioned reflexes and irrespective of training. During their daily work they make many on-the-spot decisions to safeguard the safety of their blind masters.

Reasoning Power

An amusing example of reasoning power was told to me the other day by the mother of a new baby. She had trained her dog to fetch a clean diaper from a shelf in the closet every time the baby needed to be changed. On the day of this story the infant had an upset stomach and needed changing every half hour or so. Nine times the dog made the trip to the closet and returned with the requested diaper. On the tenth trip, obviously fed up with diaper toting, he pulled all the diapers off the closet shelf and deposited them in a neat pile beside the baby's crib. He then stalked out of the room with his head high in the air.

Another example concerns a German shepherd who loved to kill rabbits. He would proudly bring home the mutilated rabbits to show them off to his master. The master was never pleased with his dog's "accomplishment" and told him so (but not very sternly) each time he arrived home with his prey. The master decided he would have to take more drastic measures to break the habit, and he next time the dog brought home a mutilated rabbit the master whipped the dog severely. The next time the dog killed a rabbit, he was found burying it, trying to hide it. Since he knew he would be punished if he came home with the dead rabbit, to me this was reasoning power, not instinct or training.

One of my patients is a very intelligent Kerry blue terrier who is always brought to my kennel for boarding when his family goes out of town. He loves the kennel and especially seems to enjoy being with all the other dogs. One time his family decided to let him stay at home with a babysitter friend while they went away for the weekend. The dog wasn't apprised of the arrangement and disappeared from the house when he saw his family drive off. While the babysitter was frantically looking for her charge, the dog was walking the three miles through town to my kennel, where he presented himself to be boarded. Another time this same dog appeared at my hospital, scratched at the door, and demandingly barked to be let in. He limped in holding up his front paw, which he had somehow cut. I examined, sutured and bandaged it, and he went on home.

INTELLIGENCE: ACUTE PERCEPTION

Telling Time of Day and Day of Week

It is an accepted fact that dogs are able to tell the time of day and also the day of the week. Just about every dog owner has at least one story to corroborate his dog's time sense.

I know a cocker spaniel who wakes his mistress every weekday at six o'clock but knows when it's Saturday and Sunday and lets her sleep later. Every evening at five he is at the bus stop to meet her, but on Friday nights she goes right from work to the beauty parlor and he knows to meet her bus at seven.

Whatever the explanation, dogs certainly do have a much more acute sense of time than most humans.

Predicting Storms

This also is a faculty that dogs are accepted as having. Sometimes hours before an impending storm they become restless and start to whine and to act in a peculiar fashion. Vibrations, rhythms, and barometric pressures beyond the threshold of human perception are felt by dogs. As a result they often "know" when a thunderstorm is coming.

INTELLIGENCE: EXTRASENSORY PERCEPTION (ESP)

Scientists believe that dogs are blessed with a sixth sense that gives them psychic powers. From time immemorial people have attributed to dogs all kinds of uncanny powers.

There have been many amazing stories of unexplainable behavior of dogs which suggest some power of premonition, some attunement with nature that is not possessed by man.

The homing instinct in dogs has been described in many

newspaper stories of dogs' returning to their old homes after traveling hundreds and even thousands of miles. ESP scientists believe that some of this ability can be accounted for through the regular senses and remembered experiences, such as territorial instincts of a dog leaving his "calling card" at various posts throughout his territory. However, behavioral scientists are attempting to get to the root of animal navigation and at the present time cannot account for all of their migratory habits. Some researchers are now agreeing that dogs do possess some powers of logic and thought deductive processes.

Some scientists believe that a dog has a built-in compass and can allow for the time of day and seasonal changes in showing his homing instincts.

It has been shown that some dogs possess more potential ESP powers than others, similar to the differences in ESP in various peoples.

One of the earliest and most famous cases of ESP concerned a dog named Prince who crossed the English channel during World War I and traveled until he found his master in the trenches in France.

ESP scientists are investigating case stories of dogs who seek and find an owner who is newly located in a place that the animal has never been. This type of story rules out any of the regular senses, as well as memory. The ability is called "psi-trailing." Hundreds of cases have been reported.

One typical case of psi-trailing involves a dog whose family moved from New York to California. The dog was left behind in New York, and eleven months later he appeared at the new home in California. This astonishing story was thoroughly checked by the scientists and passed all the tests set by the parapsychologists to authenticate it.

Dr. Joseph Banks Rhine, world famous parapsychologist at Duke University, and I exchanged many dog stories, and we both believe that a dog can sense what his master is thinking, and what his mood is, from the slightest gesture, from a fleeting facial expression. A great dog lover himself, Dr. Rhine reported to me that he had seen dogs in close harmony with their masters receive mental messages and perform feats of command without a word, a gesture, an expression, or a blinking of the eye passing between them.

Telepathy and clairvoyance predominate in the stories from Dr. Rhine's files: One story concerns an airplane accident some distance from home. At the exact moment the owner of the dog was injured in the crash, the dog started to behave in a peculiar manner and ran under the house. The master remained unconscious for several days, and during this time various members of the family tried to coax the dog out from under the house and to get him to eat, but he paid no attention to them. By flashlight they observed that his eyes were glazed and that he appeared to be in a coma. Dr. Rhine's records show that the dog came out from under the house at the exact moment his master regained consciousness; and he then appeared normal in every way.

The second story is about a little mongrel who lived with a family in Richmond, Virginia. One night the dog was at home with the family, and two of the sons were away from home on an overnight camping trip. In the middle of the night the dog started to howl in a most peculiar way. This, of course, woke the family, and as the dog had never howled before the family decided she was trying to tell them something. There didn't seem to be anything amiss in the house or around it, and yet the dog continued to howl. They became apprehensive about the boys and decided to drive out to the campsite, about ten miles away. They found the woods on fire and rapidly burning toward the boys' tent. Quick evacuation saved the boys.

Another story concerns a little terrier named Penny, who found her way in a strange place and performed an uncanny act in a cemetery. A year and a half after the death of a mother in a family, one of the daughters came home and made a visit to the graveyard. Penny was left in the car while the woman went to a water spigot in another section of the cemetery to freshen up some flowers. When the woman returned, she saw that Penny had jumped out of the car and was lying on the mother's grave whining and moaning. No other member of the family had been to the cemetery for several months, and the dog had never been there. What explanation do we mortals have for this type of behavior? How did the dog find the gravesite among the thousands of other graves?

The last story—a psi-trail case—is one of the most incredible I've ever heard. It concerns a female dog adopted by a family who found her at their summer vacation home. By the end of the summer they had become very fond of her; and they were thrilled with her new litter of puppies. Not wanting to abandon her and not being able to take a mother dog and five puppies back to their city apartment, they found a good home for her near their summer cottage. A month later the dog appeared at their apartment in New York City—thirty miles from the summer vacation home! This dog had never been to the city before, and of course had never seen their apartment. She had a puppy in her mouth; she deposited it on the apartment floor and then asked to go out. She returned the next week with a second pup and continued her trips until she had her own family and her human family under the same roof. Hard as this story is to believe, it has been completely investigated and authenticated.

All these stories prove there is a strong bond between a dog and his beloved human being—a bond that testifies to the presence of a mysterious sense in dogs that is greater in scope than we humans can imagine.

2   NORMAL BEHAVIOR AND INSTINCTS

BEHAVIORAL INFLUENCES

Behavior is never wholly inherited or wholly acquired but is always developed under the combined influences of heredity and environment. The object of socialization of a dog is to produce a well-balanced and well-adjusted animal.

The ideal dog, according to trainers, is self-assured, outgoing, and friendly with people and other dogs, with a strong pride in his own intelligence. He'll greet guests with a wag of his tail, rather than jump on them. He will not bite nor will he fight unless for the protection of himself or the family he loves. He is not overfriendly, and he is not shy. He is a "well-adjusted" dog because he has no bad personality traits that have to be corrected before he is trained.

Each dog is very much an individual and should be regarded, treated, and handled as such. If you study your dog's individual traits and mental reactions, you can train and manage him more effectively. By knowing his personality and his normal behavior patterns you will be quick to notice the slightest deviations. The normal-behaving dog is usually the happy dog. The happy dog is the product of your association with him.

It is difficult at times to establish a line of demarcation between normal and abnormal behavior of either dogs or humans. A docile little pet might turn into a ferocious tiger when being groomed or having his nails clipped. It would not be considered abnormal behavior if he were to bite his owner. This is his normal reaction to the grooming, and although he is untrained he is acting quite normal by being hostile to the person trying to perform the grooming atrocity. Usually the pet wins the battle, and his hair doesn't get combed or his nails cut. Although this is considered normal behavior, it is disconcerting to the owner to have his dog tell him when grooming is to be allowed.

17

Usually the so-called master has brought this unnatural and unpleasant state of affairs upon himself. The pet realizes that he has the upper hand and will often press his advantage. Don't underestimate these "dumb" animals. It is obvious that this dog needs some training, and most dogs actually want obedience and discipline; they respect you more if you teach and demand obedience and discipline; and they like to learn. Your dog is pleased when he masters a command and you praise him for it. It is satisfying to him to be taught to fetch things for you; he desperately wants to be needed.

His demands are so few—mainly affection and companionship. He needs to know that you like him. Treat him as an individual, praise him when he does right, punish him when he does wrong, and you are on the road to producing a normal dog. Words of praise are food to his ego, and he'll do more and more things for you for this praise. Play with him occasionally. Throw things for him to fetch, wrestle with him, and even groom him (even if he may dislike the actual grooming, he likes your spending time with him, caring for him, giving him companionship). Spend as much of your leisure time with him as possible. He lives for it, and it is a thrill for him just to be near you. This association with the greatest thing in his life—you—makes for a healthy, happy dog.

The dog is a social animal and doesn't like to be left alone. Dogs suffer from claustrophobia too. Loneliness breeds many problems. When he is not worked with, is neglected, mental deterioration sets in because of his boredom and lack of reason for being. He becomes a neurotic and unhealthy dog, much to the displeasure of everyone.

Prenatal Influences

Research has proved that environmental influences can prenatally affect the behavior of puppies. Gentle handling of the bitch during pregnancy results in the offspring's being more docile and less easily aroused by sudden disturbances in the environment. On the other hand, certain drugs given to the pregnant dog can alter the behavior of the offspring, and experimentally, electric shock to pregnant bitches results in the puppies' being more excitable.

Parturition and Postnatal Influences

The mother-puppy bond is established after normal delivery, and there is a relationship between the warmth, food, shelter-seeking behavior of the pup.

NORMAL HANDLING OF PUPPIES

In discussing normal behavior we must understand the normal handling of puppies. It is the early impressions from puppyhood that set the characteristics for future personality.

Nursing

A puppy should be handled as early as possible. During the first 3 weeks the mother usually provides all the food, warmth, and love that a puppy needs. The pattern of puppy behavior is sleeping, feeding, and playing. At the end of that time the puppy becomes receptive to the outside world, and he begins to learn. The human treatment that the puppy receives between 3 and 4 weeks of age is likely to influence its temperament as an adult. Emotional stresses such as long separations from his mother, being roughly handled or frightened by strangers, loud noises, or being left in a strange location are experiences that might have a detrimental effect on the puppy's personality.

From the 4th to the 8th week of his life the puppy begins to investigate the outside world. He learns to recognize by scent the human beings that he comes in daily contact with. He learns to recognize the voice of his caretaker, and other animals and objects that he meets every day. It is these new experiences and impressions that help to form the stability or instability of the yearling.

Most puppies raised under kennel conditions with little human contact will at five weeks show fear reactions. However, if the puppies are handled within the next 2 weeks, this fear will disappear. Puppies should be handled before 5 weeks of age; then there will be no fear reaction evident. Puppies who are not handled until after 12 weeks become increasingly timid and may be extremely difficult to catch. They can be trained but will always be more timid and less responsive than those who socialized with human beings at an earlier age.

Weaning

The period of investigation usually ends at weaning time, when the puppy is confronted with new problems. It is at this time that his intelligence develops quickly in favorable surroundings. By the time he is 3 months old a puppy can learn almost anything that is properly taught him. Even though his body may be too weak and immature to perform some of the activities he learns at this age, later in life he will show the results of his proper early education.

A properly reared puppy is happy and naturally sociable and eager to make friends. He desires patting and gentle handling and will respond favorably by growing up without fear. After weaning, a puppy should be handled by strangers and given a chance to learn that there are other gentle human beings. You should attempt to take him with you on short car trips to the market or shopping center so that he can get accustomed to the car and to city noises. He has to learn that these will not harm him. An animal learns by association and repetition. The more often he's exposed to tenderness and love, the more favorable will be his impression of human beings. A puppy must be encouraged at an early age to form his own impressions and must have confidence in human beings.

A puppy's basic instinct is to love and be loved. However, if he suffers an unhappy puppyhood, his love for the human race can turn to anxiety and distrust. We then have a problem dog.

The Orphan

Although dog psychologists say that a puppy should be put into a new home between the ages of 6 and 8 weeks and that any time after 12 weeks the dog is likely to be maladjusted, I am still old-fashioned enough to believe that dogs can adjust to a new family life at any age if they are basically of sound disposition. I know of countless cases where a close and mutual relationship has resulted from the adoption of dogs of all ages. Many strays have made wonderful family pets. Daily, people adopt dogs of all ages from animal shelters and dog pounds, and good master-pet associations are achieved. In raising an adult dog, as in raising a puppy, tender loving care goes a long way in establishing a firm relationship. But it must be emphasized that disposition is of primary importance in choosing a puppy or an adult dog.

DISTINCTIVE BEHAVIOR OF BREED

Certain breeds have distinct inherited physical and behavioral characteristics which are bred from generation to generation. The guard dogs (Doberman pinscher and German shepherd) have a strong body with a great desire for territorial defense, and so they make excellent watchdogs. It is interesting to watch these puppies as they begin to assume protective custody of both the house they live in and their human family. Although this is natural instinct and cannot be taught, it can be developed as the dogs mature.

Hunting dogs, because of their keen eyesight and keen sense of smell, have been bred for years to various game. The Saluki hound and the whippet, because of their great speed, can catch their game. The larger breeds, such as Irish wolfhound and Scottish deerhound, see their game. The bird dogs, such as spaniels, setters, pointers, and retrievers, also hunt by eyesight but primarily employ the sense of smell. The hound breeds, such as bloodhound, English foxhound, and beagle, hunt mainly by scent, with their noses close to the ground. Small breeds, such as terriers, were originally trained to hunt rodents. They are aggressive and quick and go after their prey assertively. Dachshunds were bred for hunting badgers, and their body and leg formation makes them ideally suited for catching their particular quarry.

Breed selection has given rise to a large variety of dogs,

and each dog, through generations, has been bred for distinct physical and behavioral characteristics. Some dogs have been highly trained in a specialized way for specific jobs—for example, the German shepherd as guide dog for the blind, in police work, and for the armed forces—each requiring specialized training and certain characteristics.

Through the years dogs have come to be adopted more and more for companionship, and for this purpose a small, easily controlled pet is the most practical type. Most people want an affectionate dog, easily trained, not too aggressive, and not vicious or destructive. For them the small or medium-sized dog is the most suitable.

TEMPERAMENTAL DIFFERENCES WITHIN BREED

There can be great differences in temperament in the same breed due to breeding. For instance, although the German shepherd is a watchdog and working dog by heritage, he may become unpredictable, aggressive, or shy because of indiscriminate inbreeding. Through inbreeding many breeds are becoming disoriented from their original purpose. Years ago cocker spaniels were hurt to some extent by indiscriminate breeding—by the lure of profit and of developing champion dogs. Another prime example is the poodle, currently enjoying great popularity. To make quick and easy money, much inbreeding and unselective breeding are going on, producing and reproducing undesirable traits and physical anomalies. To continue at the present pace may spell doom to the breed.

INSTINCTS

Your dog has many curiosities and strange instincts which are inheritances from thousands of years of life in the world. In reality you have a breath of the wild in your home, still retaining traces of the days when his ancestors roamed the woods, matching wits and courage with wild boars and tigers. One of his curiosities is his nose: it is split into a backward curve and trembles with sensitiveness. Keenness of scent was especially necessary to the primitive dog. Incidentally, he always slept with his nose pointed upward to catch the scent of enemies approaching, which involved walking in circles to catch the proper direction of the wind before bedding down. As you've no doubt noticed, the dog still walks in circles before lying down.

The Maternal Instinct

One of the basic instincts is the mother-pup relationship. The mother acts in an instinctive manner; thought processes are not involved. The mother cares for the young, and the father, in some cases, assists, depending on how much motherly instinct he has inherited. In the wild state the father helped rear the puppies, but the domestication process has eliminated him from this role.

The maternal instinct is a prominent factor in raising puppies. One of the earliest signs of this instinct is nest-making before the onset of whelping. The licking and eating of the placenta by the bitch seems to be a necessary preliminary to the cleaning of the young. It also seems to be the basis of the maternal attachment to the offspring; experience has shown that if the bitch is prevented from cleaning and eating the placenta, the usual close link between mother and puppy is not formed. Quite normally the bitch will push aside sick and dying puppies and will sometimes even bury them.

Normally the bitch tends the litter and stays close for about 3 weeks. Then gradually she leaves the box more and more. She will clean the puppies by licking them and by ingesting the urine and feces until they are about 4 weeks old; by then they have been taught to leave the box to take care of their elimination. At about 3 weeks she starts their training period; she punishes them, growls at them, knocks them over. At the onset of the weaning period, by way of introducing her puppies to solid food, she regurgitates her food for them. The bitch begins to lose her maternal affection when the puppies begin taking solid food, at around 4 to 5 weeks.

Puppies are blind until about 9 or 10 days old. Since they cannot see, they stay snuggled close to the mother's warm breast. In the wild, with sight, many of these puppies would have wandered off and quickly perished.

Litters usually have one particularly rough member, and there will often be a tendency to fight. These slight altercations can be considered normal.

An interesting phenomenon in dogs, which is also seen in humans, is that no matter how roughly a mother treats her young before weaning, the suckling retains its love and affection for her.

The Maternal Instinct Altered or Inhibited. The normal maternal instincts may be altered somewhat in a bitch who is over-attached to her owner or has been reared as an indulged "perpetual puppy." She may be deficient in maternal behavior and refuse to nurse her offspring. Such a bitch should have her owner close by when she whelps and in the subsequent nursing procedures. There should be no strangers present during this period, as she may be thrown into hysterics and harm her puppies, or even kill and eat them.

The maternal instinct may be inhibited in some dogs when there is a Caesarean section. When they awake from the anesthetic, some of them are indifferent to their puppies and will even harm them. This is not a general rule fortunately, but you should be all means stay with the bitch while her newborn puppies are given to her.

The maternal instinct can be affected by hormonal imbalance. Sometimes there will be no breast formation or milk for the puppies, although there may be a normal delivery.

Always, if the bitch is emotionally disturbed about her puppies, or indifferent, the puppies should be removed from her and raised by hand, both because of the harm that might befall them and because it is easy for them to assume some of her emotional unstableness. With hand raising they can be normal puppies in all traits and not inherit the mother's tendency toward indifference to maternal responses.

The Care-Giving Instinct

This is an aspect of the maternal mother-pup relationship which involves instinctive action. The mother dog sometimes engages in an advanced type of social behavior—a grooming which is a toothful combing for fleas or foxtails either in her young, in another dog, or in her master. We often see a dog "groom" someone in her human family or a canine playmate. She will lick the ears and neck in an affectionate way which is her expression of extreme love. This is her desire to mother her human family.

The Suckling Instinct

This, of course, is a strong instinct. If puppies are not suckled by the mother, there should be some substitute. Even a pacifier will do. However, it is best to use a bottle with a small opening so that the puppy will have to work to get the milk out. If a puppy is not allowed to suck, a non-nutritional sucking habit will sometimes develop and persist in later life.

The Sexual Instinct

Domestication has so relaxed the dog's morals that today's concept of the dog is that he will breed with any female. Not unlike their human counterparts, male dogs play the gallant to every bitch in heat, even complete strangers.

When puppies are about 4 weeks old, some sexual activity will be noted—there will be some copulatory movement—but the phase lasts only about 2 weeks and then disappears until sexual maturity.

In the male dog the raising of the hind leg is usually hormonally controlled and is not learned by the pup from other male dogs. The male hormones affect the behavior of the male dog. There is also a strong link between the sexual urge of the male and the hormonal smell of the female urine. Male dogs are attracted to female dogs in heat by the odor of their urine and instinctively know when the bitch is ready for breeding.

Normal Sexual Behavior

Puppies are like children in early stimulations and sexual sensations. The mother licks her puppies, stimulating the genitals and other sensitive areas. Litter mates rub against one another and their mother for pleasurable sensations. During early growth long before sexual maturity, they have oral and bodily contact during which they exhibit sexual excitement. There is no differentiation between the sexes—males ride males and females are stimulated by females. This is normal behavior and is not considered homosexuality until sexual maturity. If the animal does not change after sexual maturity, it remains a homosexual the rest of its life.

Sex play or forepleasure is normal in dogs and important in breeding. The mating pair should be put in a room by themselves and allowed to undergo the pleasure of sex play. It is stimulating to both sexes, and often an aggressive romantic male can win over a latently frigid female.

During normal sex play dogs lick one another around the sensitive areas: penis, vulva, clitoris, nipples, anus, lips, mouth, tongue, eyelids, ears. Often the female will roll over on her back like a puppy and allow the male to lick the smooth and tender (usually hairless) skin on her abdomen, thighs, and elbow regions. Sometimes the male will allow the female to ride him, and this may enable her to have an orgasm. The normal female doesn't usually have an orgasm at the time of copulation but may have one during the foreplay, while riding the male.

Frequently when a female in heat is kept from male dogs, she will become so sexually aroused during the middle of her estrus cycle that she will ride other females to try to satisfy her sexual needs. Likewise, males cooped up for long periods without female companionship will ride one another. After returning to normal conditions, most dogs will return to heterosexuality and enjoy the normal pleasures of sexual contact.

The Signature of the Dog. The habit dogs have of smelling one another under their tails is a normal instinct called the "signature" of the dog. It has to do with the odor that is eliminated from the anal glands. Under severe emotional stress, and fear, evacuation of these glands can occur, and the odor is quite putrid. These are the same anal sacs that are used as a defensive mechanism in the skunk.

There are some who believe that the anal-sac secretions may be a source of sexual attraction. The hypothesis is that the secretions of the anal sac contain the hormonal odors depicting the sexual period of the female.

The Herding-Roaming Instinct

The dog is born with an urge to roam and form packs. We should all try to prevent our pets from traveling with a pack, because this is when dogs revert to the call of the wild. They usually get into trouble by attacking other dogs and animals and even people. It is normal for a male during the mating season to join with a group of dogs and follow the trail of any female in heat.

Communication Between Dogs

There are many normal communication patterns between dogs. When danger is threatening, there is a certain posture to a dog's body. He has a distinctive way of slinking when he is submitting to a new threat. When his tail is between his legs, he is submitting to a danger. Raising his paw is a sign of submission.

Urinary scent is one of the commonest ways dogs communicate with one another. The male dog uses this device for marking his territory, as does the female dog. It is normal behavior for territorial rights.

Vocalization is another means of communication, and it varies from breed to breed. Some breeds, like the hound, howl, while some small terrier types are yappy. Guard dogs bark to let both people and animals know that they are protecting their territory. Hunting dogs bay to express themselves.

Only tame or domesticated dogs bark. Wild dogs and wolves don't bark; they howl. Barking is an imitation. As the master urged him with shouts to go after game the dog in his excitement imitated these sounds and in time developed the barking habit.

The scientific explanation of howling in the domestic dog is that it is merely the outcropping of instincts developed through the ages when wild dogs hunted in packs; the howl was their rallying call.

The dog still retains many of his primitive instincts, but these impulses can be guided through training and education, and we can mold our dog into the temperament and personality type we want. He wants to be taught and is eager to learn. It is up to us to teach him.

3 TRAINING FOR NORMAL BEHAVIOR

FIRST PRINCIPLES

It must be evident by now that it is next to impossible to have a normal, well-behaved, even-tempered dog without discipline and some training. Once a dog is trained he is a better pet and a greater source of pride, and he himself is happier for knowing that his master is pleased with him.

There are many books devoted to discipline and training which are well worth reading. There are also many fine obedience-training classes throughout the country, and I heartily recommend this form of training. Of course, you must be willing to accept the fact that if your dog fails the course and becomes a dropout it is entirely your fault, not the dog's. He is a willing subject; it is your responsibility to help him become an apt pupil.

Any sincerely interested dog owner can train his own dog, and it can be a most rewarding education for both master and pupil. Patience and plenty of self-control are the most important ingredients for successful training. At times you have to be firm, you have to be gentle, you have to scold, and you have to praise. You must temper punishment with praise. You and your dog must share mutual love and confidence, and your seriousness of purpose must be sincere.

Basically dog training is built on reward and punishment. A kind word or a caress makes any dog feel that he is pleasing his master. Other meaningful gestures of affection that a dog can understand are taking his muzzle playfully in both hands, rubbing him behind his ears, rubbing your hand gently over his flanks and back, or taking his nose in your hand affectionately. A pat on his head, running his ear through your hand, or just the words "Good dog" make for a happy, grateful dog.

Men and women alike can be trainers, but there is a tendency in women to be less strong and authoritative in their commands than men and less stern in their punishment. Just the same, some of the best obedience trainers in the country are women, because they have a way of giving commands that dogs seem to like and pay attention to. So I appeal to you women to be strict and to follow up your training with stern enough punishment when the dog doesn't obey.

My answer to the frequent question, What is the best age at which to start training a dog? is 3 months for minor commands and a minimum of 6 months for any intensive training. Don't start too early, for a puppy can easily be intimidated. Too severe training and discipline can destroy his confidence and attachment and have a permanent affect on his personality. Severe punishment, rough handling, loud and harsh words can turn the puppy into a distrustful pet full of antagonisms toward the human race. Start slowly and gently in training the puppy, and use incentive and praise.

Most puppies form a strong attachment to an individual human being which may persist or wane, and there is often a phase of adolescent independence when the dog will become disobedient and defiant—just like a teen-ager. Discipline is needed during this critical period, but it must be mixed with patience and must not be overbearing.

Although it can be too early to start training, it is never too late. I don't for one moment believe that you can't teach an old dog new tricks. He can be taught new tricks and all the basic commands whatever his age. It is bound to be a little more difficult to break old habits like barking, chasing cars, and sleeping on satin cushions, but here too, with perseverance, new tricks can replace old habits.

I don't intend to get into the fine points of discipline and training, but I will briefly discuss the rudiments of normal behavior.

Your dog must be relaxed before you begin a training session. He can't learn while he is tense and timid and in a nervous state. If he is confused and defiant, he will subconsciously resist your teaching. Complete relaxation is essential to successful dog training.

GET TO KNOW YOUR DOG

To train your dog to the best advantage of both of you, you must get to know him. For example, there are sensitive dogs who squeal at the slightest slap with the disciplinary newspaper, the merest jerk of the training lead, or even the touch of a grooming comb. A word of ridicule, to hurt his feelings, should be enough to bring him into line.

Then there's the pesty dog. He's the aggressive type who is always pushing himself at you for your attention. He jumps on your guests, nuzzles them, brings a ball to be thrown. This dog needs special firmness and sternness to rid him of his overdemanding trait. He's basically good, but he has to be taught that he's not number one in the world. He's the type of dog that if allowed to will take over the entire family and run the whole show. He usually has to be taken down a peg or two before any good training habits can be evolved.

If your dog is shy, he must not be overpunished. I would give exaggerated praise and patting when he does something right and gentle but firm correction when he does something wrong. It is possible for the shy dog to learn, and learning will improve his personality by allowing him to gain confidence in himself.

Various breeds require different kinds and degrees of punishment. For instance, in beagles mild punishment is usually enough to inhibit undesirable activities. However, in a larger dog, such as collie or German shepherd, your punishment most likely will have to be more severe physically because the determination to resist you will probably be stronger.

You have to know your dog's personality when you are training him because each dog has to be handled differently. Each animal has a threshold of sensitivity which you must determine in order to know how far you need to jerk the leash for response. Train him according to his temperament and anticipate his next move.

GETTING THE MESSAGE ACROSS

Anyone can train his dog so long as the animal is able to understand what he is being taught. It's strictly a matter of communication. That he loves you and wants to please you is a big plus factor on your side in learning how to train him. As with people—getting on the same level when you want to communicate with them—so it is with dogs. You have to get down on your haunches, crouch beside your dog, and win his confidence. Talk "man to man" with him, in quiet, soft tones.

I can't overemphasize that you should constantly talk to your dog while training him. But please don't raise your voice, or shout, or yell, or scream. And don't, for goodness' sake, lose your temper and kick at him or throw things at him. He'll not only be frightened and confused, but he's liable to lose some of his respect for you. If you feel a fit of temper coming on, dismiss the class forthwith!

Your dog can tell by the tone of your voice whether you mean the command. He has to know you mean it; he has to be convinced. Don't be wishy-washy; your dog will understand your tone of voice better than he will understand words. Try to develop voice tones that will convey the meaning of your commands. He will learn the significance of your voice tones and ultimately the meanings of some words.

In getting the message across, word commands have to be augmented by body contact so that the dog can associate the two. By repeating the body contacts with the same words, he will soon learn what you are trying to tell him. I advocate a choke collar; it is one of the few ways of communicating your message. (It is not a cruel instrument and can be used on the smallest and most fragile dog when handled properly and gently.) In time, when he understands your message, your voice commands will suffice. It is a matter of repetition until he understands what you want. The whole aim of training is to teach the animal to react to your voice commands and hand signals.

For disobedience and discipline, sometimes words such as "Bad dog" or "Phooey" are enough, but for some strong-minded individuals I am not against discipline with a rolled-up newspaper or a switch, or in some really tough dogs, a leather strap. Although it may be necessary to give stiff physical correction now and then, remember never to hold a grudge in training. Follow up an admonishment with a reward or praise for some other deed. It will encourage your pet to do better next time.

Failure to respond to his master's wishes is usually due to confusion or to physical illness or incapability. Patience and understanding can correct all but physical inability.

One of the strongest methods of punishing a dog is to grab him by the scruff of the neck and shake him. This goes back to primitive days when dogs roamed in packs and the leader punished an errant follower by grabbing him by the neck and shaking him severely. This technique, although not practiced much nowadays, is still an effective way of making a dog feel bad. He knows that he is really being punished when you shake him by the scruff.

MAKE THE LESSONS ENJOYABLE

Dogs get bored with long training sessions. If you work with them over 20 minutes at a time, they will lose interest and stop listening to you. For a younger dog or a puppy, 5 to 10 minutes is long enough for any one training session. But do it frequently, and don't punish him if he does something wrong. When he does well, praise him, give him a reward. And make the rewards worthwhile—favorite tidbits. If he does badly, a verbal "Bad dog" is usually enough. Vary the lessons and intersperse the hard things with easy and known commands—and make them as much fun as possible.

BE CONSISTENT

Dogs are constantly observing their masters, trying to figure out what is wanted of them. Be consistent in your requests and responses, and be consistent in your aims and methods, so as not to confuse or deceive. Follow up the same learning procedures with the same praise, reward, or disapproval response. And don't let the dog get away with something one time and punish him another time—you'll just bewilder him.

TEACH RESPECT

A dog has to be taught to respect his master. He automatically will love you out of his respect for you. You have to be his master, not let him be yours. He wants to know what you, as his master and teacher, expect of him. As you communicate your wishes and he learns to understand you, he will forever be your loyal follower and try to please you. Once the dog knows his master is the leader, he will be a happy follower.

As well as the five fundamental training points, there are five basic commands which I believe all dogs should be taught. They are Heel, Sit, Down, Stay, and Come.

BASIC COMMANDS

Heel. You teach your dog to walk on your left side without pulling in front of you; he is always to walk in back of you, at your left heel. When he tries to get in front of you, you jerk the choke collar while repeating, "Heel."

Sit. You will pull the leash straight up with your right hand while pressing on his hindquarters with your left hand, repeating the word "Sit."

Down. You grasp the leash under the dog's neck and push straight down on it while holding the other end of the leash in your right hand. The voice command should have a downward inflection. Sometimes in a stubborn animal it's necessary to pull the front legs forward to weaken his support and then pull down on the collar as you say, "Down."

Stay. You put your dog in a sitting position and push gently against his chest or nose if he tries to move forward. You command him to stay and move slowly from him. Keep repeating, "Stay" as you gradually increase the distance between you.

Come. Be sure to do this with a leash or a long rope. First put him on the "Stay" command. Use the word "Come" with an inviting tone and inflection and give the leash a little tug toward you. When he gets to you, praise him or reward him.

I can't in all conscience end this chapter without a word of sympathy for the weak owners—and I include myself—who sneak bits of food to their dogs under the table, reward them with a cookie for every little expression of affection or funny-ism, or let them get away with all kinds of "favored" idiosyncrasies. Hopefully we can manage to exert enough training and discipline to keep our permissiveness and our dogs' "advantages" within bounds.

4   ABNORMAL BEHAVIOR: THE NEUROTIC DOG

We are seeing an increasing number of nervous dogs in our midst. While some of these dogs owe their nervousness to inherited faults of temperament, most of them owe it to a variety of unfavorable environmental conditions. From their normal primitive ways we have changed dogs' normal behavior patterns so much in recent years that it is small wonder their neuroses are increasing apace. Also, because dogs imitate their masters closely, and unfortunately even the bad aspects, they seem to be acquiring many of the neuroses and mental ailments of the human race.

I feel obliged to interject that not all owners of misbehaving nuisance pets are maladjusted. Most of these owners are nice people who just happen to be victims of circumstance. They own a juvenile delinquent dog and can't bear the thought of parting with it. It is to these victimized dog owners that most of this chapter is dedicated. It will discuss ways and means of handling problem dogs.

At a renowned clinic for mentally ill dogs, in Copenhagen, last year alone more than 2,000 mentally disturbed dogs from all over Europe received treatment. Patients are usually fit to return to their owners in about a month—although it takes up to 3 months to cure canines addicted to tranquilizers. A high proportion of the disturbed dogs are sent to the clinic to be cured of biting people. "Dogs that bite children or handicapped people," theorizes Arne Soerensen, founder of the clinic, "are not necessarily mean, but frightened when pushed up to a small child or a stranger."

CAUSES OF ABNORMAL BEHAVIOR

Inherited Nervousness

Although most cases of nervousness are basically due to environmental factors, some dogs do inherit the tendency. If a nervous dog was bred from two non-nervous parents, then we can be fairly certain that the nervousness is environmental. Inherited nervousness should be eliminated from the strain by not allowing such dogs to breed; they should be castrated or spayed. Behavioral abnormalities that should be watched for before allowing an animal to breed are excessive timidity and fear of strangers; refusal to leave a familiar environment; sound, touch, and sight shyness; fear-biting; fear of sudden changes; and excessive activity. Any of these traits would be inherited in offspring and establish and compound many abnormal traits.

The vast majority of descendants of the shy, fear-biting bitch will shy at friendly animals even though the sires are normal and friendly creatures. Furthermore, in addition to the direct inheritance of shyness, the behavior of the mother is likely to teach the puppies to react violently, as she does, to strangers and other disturbing influences. Nor is this shyness modified by training.

Physical Disorders

When I examine a dog that is brought to me because of abnormal behavior, there are many factors that I consider. We must always investigate the possibility of a physical disorder as the cause of any abnormal behavior before we can incriminate a mental problem. Many times the animal doesn't feel well and acts in a peculiar manner because of an organic problem. I usually give the animal a complete physical checkup, looking for one of the following disorders which can affect behavior: worms, thyroid disease, a spinal-disc disorder, poisoning, constipation, diarrhea, urinary ailments, allergic reactions, milk fever in a nursing bitch, sex-organ malfunction, anal-gland infection. Many diseases, such as rabies, spinal meningitis, distemper, and epilepsy, can cause abnormal behavior. Brain tumors, abscesses, and such traumatic things as a blow to the head or an inner-ear infection can cause abnormal behavior and even affect a dog's temperament. I have seen dogs with head injuries undergo such abnormal behavior as loss of social and sexual drives, loss of hunting tendencies, and complete lethargy, and I've seen them regress to puppy habits and further—back to the point of primitive wild canine behavior. Sometimes a good-natured animal will turn vicious and unreliable. After elimination of the organic problem, the abnormal behavior generally will clear up.

An overdose of tranquilizers or sedatives will change behavior. Some drugs accumulate in the blood stream and gradually over a period of time will cause a derangement in mental abilities. If the dog becomes dopy or sleepy, or acts stupid under certain medication, have your veterinarian check it out to make sure there are no sedatives in it that are affecting the dog's ability.

A dog behaving abnormally can conceivably be under the influence of alcohol, especially around Christmas time, when always at least one pet is brought to us who has consumed too much eggnog. At a recent veterinary convention there was a discussion about the increase in the number of alcoholic dogs. You can tell when a dog is hung over; he's bleary-eyed and listless and looks like he's got a headache. However, he can't get the stuff himself; someone has to give it to him. The drinking generally starts as a gag at a party, when someone gets the dog to lap up some booze. He takes a liking to the stuff and becomes a sneaky party drinker.

Unsuitable Environment—Undesirable Youthful Experiences

If a puppy is reared in seclusion or in an unsuitable environment, he may be expected to grow up to be unhappy, nervous, and timid. When he's confronted with a new situation, he sometimes goes to pieces. He doesn't know how to cope with new problems. If he's under 3 months of age, he can easily be taught to deal with crises. The older he is, the more difficult it will be and the slower his response to treatment. The one thing that all dogs of any age respond to is tender loving care. It takes a lot of patience and consideration to deal with the problem dog. The pet has to first of all believe in you as an individual and trust you as the one person in his life. He's more apt to do what you want if he has this confidence.

There are certain conditions in the family life of an owner that can affect a dog's behavior: a tense and stressful family life, a shy owner, a fearful owner, an anxious owner, a tense owner, an excessively permissive owner, a bored owner, and a person who isolates himself, such as an introvert.

In order to suggest an atmosphere of family life, one progressive kennel owner pipes in radio soap operas to comfort homesick dogs. Experts have discovered that matronly voices and gruff but friendly voices of middle-aged men have a soothing effect on dogs.

So remember, if music fails to soothe your bored and lonesome dog, let him hear some radio soap operas.

The Aging Process

Senility affects the various organs of the body, so as the dog gets older there will be a slow, gradual change in some of his behavior patterns. His toilet training is one of the earliest things to go. Where he was once well housebroken, we get an animal who begins to dribble urine—much to his embarrassment. The muscles of the bladder gradually lose their control. Certain kidney diseases, such as nephritis, and also diabetes can cause the dog to wet through inability to hold urine. Sometimes it would seem that an animal is being spiteful and getting even with his owner by wetting the floor, and this does happen, but most of the time it's a physical problem. In older dogs have your veterinarian check the kidneys at periodic intervals. As the male dog gets older his prostate gland often enlarges and produces an inflammation which causes him to urinate often. It is painful and needs medical attention.

In an older dog you will usually notice a loss in hearing. At first it is very gradual, and you may not realize that he is having trouble hearing you. As he deafens you might use high-pitched sounds, such as whistles, rather than voice commands.

Cataracts form in older eyes, and your dog may have trouble recognizing you. There is a gradual graying and loss of vision, accompanied by changing behavior patterns.

In the older dog you may notice a change in his attitudes

toward the members of his human family. Although he still loves them dearly, he wants his comfort and solitude more often. He wants to be left alone instead of romping and playing as he once did. This is not of his desire but because of his physical disabilities. It will be easier for him if you can adapt to his dilemma and be sympathetic and patient with him. As long as he is near you, he is happy. Of course, like older people, he may sometimes get a little irritable and not want to be handled. Accede to his demands. He has been and still is your loyal companion.

NEUROTIC MANIFESTATIONS

It is the consensus of the experts that the tensions of our modern-day civilization have a deteriorating effect on our pets.

The present-day neurotic dog is unfortunately a development of easy living, particularly in homes where he is coddled or, at the opposite extreme, where the people attempting to train him use such overbearing methods that they cow the puppy and make him mentally timid and frightened.

Other causes of neuroticism among dogs are loneliness, lack of exercise, lack of proper training, and overfeeding.

In describing a neurotic dog I would say that most of the time he is restless. He whines and whimpers, and barks excessively. He is not dependable when strangers are in the vicinity; he doesn't like their presence, and if they come near him he is apt to snap at them without warning. The neurotic dog is usually a finicky eater; overfeeding and too frequent feeding have helped to make some neurotic dogs what they are. It's best to keep certain neurotic dogs slightly hungry so that they'll respond to commands with more obedience, in anticipation of a reward of food.

Psychosomatic Ailments

Psychosomatic ailments are a form of abnormal dog behavior. They're closely allied to emotional reactions and are resorted to as a means of gaining attention. These animals aren't faking a sickness—they are actually ill. Various emotions are responsible for psychosomatic illnesses, but the outstanding one seems to be jealously. Psychosomatic ailments are actual organic ailments of which emotional factors are a cause. They can range anywhere from sexual maladjustment to human beings to animal self-mutilation and suicide. Psychosomatic medicine is a fairly new field in veterinary medicine, and in certain cases of emotionally caused physical disabilities help can be instituted.

Discovering the cause of each emotional ailment is a special challenge to every veterinarian. An interesting case I had involved a dog brought to me with a seemingly incurable skin condition. The poor dog scratched constantly. The owners had used everything from burnt cylinder oil to highly refined cortisone preparations without effect. While I was questioning the master, it came to light that there had been no skin trouble or scratching until a cat had joined the household. We checked the dog for sensitization to cat hairs but found none. We then decided to work on the theory that the dog was jealous of the cat and scratched to gain attention. When a new home was found for the cat, the dog's skin condition promptly cleared up—and no medication was necessary.

In an effort to gain attention dogs have done some strange things, but the queerest case I ever have seen is a male dachshund who goes into psychosomatic labor pains when his mate is about to have puppies. The male resents his mate's being the center of attraction whenever motherhood is imminent. In order to get into the act he goes through labor pains with his mate. He climbs into the whelping box with her and grunts and groans and strains and carries on like the real thing. As each puppy is born he cleans and attends to it. At the completion of whelping the mother dog chases him out of the box and takes over her puppies. This pair has had several litters, and the male has behaved similarly each time.

Asthmatic Seizures

Asthma seems to be an ailment of emotional origin. I have seen dogs that were jealous of either a human or another dog go into loud asthmatic wheezing when things weren't going their way and they wanted to gain attention. Some excitable dogs will have a seizure when the doorbell rings and strangers come into the house.

With a seizure the animal works himself into a frenzy and begins to pant and to breathe with loud gasps. Sometimes his tongue turns blue; and some dogs faint from lack of oxygen. Medically the bronchial tubes become constricted, and the dogs can't get enough oxygen into their lungs.

The best treatment for a dog in this state is to pick him up, talk to him, soothe him, and relax him; soon the breathing will return to normal. Some animals have to be kept on respiratory sedatives or tranquilizers to prevent recurrence of these attacks. In preventing attacks, when you expect a lot of people in your house, or neighborhood children playing nearby, I advise giving the animal some sedation, for asthmatic bronchial attacks can prove fatal if the dog has a weak heart.

The short-nosed breeds, such as bulldog, Boston terrier, pug, and Pekingese, are the prime victims of this ailment.

Loss of Appetite

Loss of appetite can be a psychosomatic ailment, especially when the dog is obviously on a hunger strike. Almost any dog in new surroundings may refrain from eating the first day. However, if after 2 or 3 days the animal still is not eating, it is usually due to emotional trauma. For example, a dog's feelings can be hurt when you put him in a boarding kennel as you go off on a trip. He feels left out, unwanted, unloved. Most normal dogs will go right to food as soon as something is presented to them to their liking. The psychosomatic dog who will not eat usually shows other symptomatic signs, such as hiding in a corner, involuntary urination and defecation, resistance to handling or walking with the new sitters, and a fearful attitude, with the whites of his eyes showing.

Even in their own familiar home, there are some dogs who won't eat if everything isn't perfectly in place, or when there's company, even though their owners are near.

Loss of Bowel or Bladder Control

Severe emotional stress, anxiety, or shock can produce loss of bowel or urine control in almost any animal. This is expected and normal. However, there are mentally disturbed animals who lose bowel or urine control without any apparent cause. In such a disturbed dog anything that is not to his liking can produce these ailments.

Pseudopregnancy, or False Pregnancy

This is a fairly common psychosomatic ailment, and it is frustrating to both dog and owner. The dog is definitely affected physically; she becomes very uncomfortable, with large swollen breasts full of lactating milk dripping from her nipples. Some animals drip milk wherever they lie down and continue lactation during the 4- to 6-week normal nursing period. Often they will stop eating and lose a lot of weight.

Some females at the time of delivery give all the signs of impending whelping. The vagina becomes enlarged, and there is a discharge. I've seen them go through false labor pains, tearing up newspapers and making a bed just as if they were preparing for puppies. During the period for nursing their puppies they usually stay in bed, or lie under chairs and other objects, and even refuse to eat. They have the maternal instinct of a nursing mother and will frequently carry objects (rubber toys, shoes, pillows) around in their mouths and snuggle them close to their breasts to simulate puppies. They are suspicious, protective, and disagreeable to anyone who goes near. At times they get upset and depressed, looking for their puppies.

Why the female does this, no one seems to know, but we do know how to treat it—to relieve the poor bitch of her feverish breasts, her anxiety over her "puppies," and her depressed state. She definitely needs treatment. Your veterinarian can treat her with hormones; and if there is fever, with antibiotics; and if she's emotionally upset, he will use tranquilizers to calm her down. I believe in applying camphorated oil to the breasts. Just apply it lightly to the nipples, and it will relieve the pain and dry up the milk; don't rub or massage it, as it will stimulate the milk flow. Some bitches self-nurse, and this is a disagreeable development which prolongs both the physical and mental anguish. When there's a profuse flow of milk, these bitches can be used as wet nurses to orphan puppies.

As well as medication, there should be a lot of tender loving care. Give the bitch as much love as she will allow. Don't punish her if she growls at you. Be patient and gentle.

There is disagreement between veterinarians and research scientists on whether false pregnancy is an emotional disorder or strictly a hormonal malfunction. I believe that there is an imbalance of hormones in the body, with a consequent emotional change in the animal. There's no supportive evidence that false pregnancy is hereditary. Usually if a bitch has one attack, she will be susceptible to further pseudopregnancies. Such animals may have to be spayed; they are undesirable as breeders. However, for those who had intended to breed a dog, I would advise trying to breed her at least once. Sometimes having a litter of puppies will straighten out the hormonal disorder. But if it's not successful, I would advise a hysterectomy. It will prolong the health and happiness of the animal, for she does suffer terrible physical and mental anguish during false pregnancy.

Occasionally during false pregnancy a bitch will work out her own solution. A dog I know, a devoted member of family, became jealous when her mistress had a baby—the first baby. While the mistress was nursing her baby, the dog developed a false pregnancy, filled up with milk, and tried to cuddle many objects around the house. However, her makeshift puppies were not satisfactory, so she went out looking for living objects to suckle. She came home one day with three baby rabbits, put them into her bed and began nursing them.

Fortunately jealousy of a new baby in a household works itself out in ways such as the above. Usually the dog will accept the baby as part of the family and lie by its crib and protect it.

When the baby starts crawling, the dog will play with it. I have never heard of a dog harming a baby or willfully injuring a baby because of jealousy.

Sexual Disorders

There are many psychosomatic sexual disorders. Even with two normal dogs the mating process is a strained one for our home-grown pets—those who don't roam the streets breeding with any dog that comes along. In some of our planned breedings tension and excitement will occasionally prevent dogs from getting together. There are some emotionally disturbed pets, those who have been spoiled by overpermissive owners, who show little inclination to mate with their own species, and the females often make poor mothers even if they are bred. Many overdependent females are so attached to their human masters that they will be frigid to the point of being vicious to the male attempting to mate. A spoiled male may not show any desire to breed and even upon stimulation will show impotence. Sometimes a male dog who has been raised with an older female who has dominated him will show no inclination to normal mating.

It is well known that miscarriages can occur because of emotional trauma. In highly excitable dogs almost any disturbing event can cause premature whelping. In such dogs puppies sometimes arrive without the accompanying normal flow of milk. The bitch sometimes will refuse to care for the puppies and may even kill and eat them. The theory behind this is that she fears someone will hurt her puppies. In my opinion there's also the possibility that she feels disdain for the puppies and an unwillingness to share family affection with them.

Car Sickness

Although car sickness is usually caused by an inner-ear disturbance, motion sickness can sometimes be classified as psychosomatic in origin because some carsick-prone dogs begin to drool and show nausea before they get into the car. It is controlled by emotional factors.

This ailment can be helped and controlled with anti-motion-sickness pills or tranquilizers to calm the anxiety of the dog before he gets into the car. If the dog has a tendency toward drooling or nausea, a drug such as dramamine or bonamine, with a tranquilizer, is advisable. In my opinion the tranquilizer is more important than the dramamine or bonamine because it's fear of the car that makes the animal drool.

Animals can be trained not to be fearful of a car. Of course, it's easier if done in early puppyhood—taking the puppy for short rides (preferably on any empty stomach). Some dogs are taken in the car only to the veterinarian or to the boarding kennel, and as these places are often distasteful to the dog, the association can be unfortunate and traumatic. It's good to take him on rides for pure enjoyment, with something he likes to do as part of the trip—a run in the woods, a food treat.

OTHER NEUROTICISMS

Claustrophobia

Just like humans, dogs are subject to claustrophobia. Some dogs during and after confinement show abnormal behavior patterns. One manifestation is tail chasing; the dog chases his tail continuously until he collapses from exhaustion. Another is spot attacking. The dog stares rigidly at a spot on the floor for about five minutes and then springs into the air to attack the spot. He will repeat this behavior continually while in confinement. Claustrophobia is offset by giving the dog some freedom and exercise.

Antisocial Tendencies

These tendencies can vary all the way from seeming disdain for association with other animals to active association with humans only.

Anxiety

Anxiety is a neuroticism dogs acquire from humans. The symptoms are restlessness and rapid or loud panting. The anxiety can become so intense that the animal loses control of his bowels and bladder.

Compulsive Behavior

Much of the dog's behavior is compulsive, and so long as his uncontrollable desires are not harmful or vicious, they usually don't present problems. Behavior is easily learned and tolerated in a dog; he enjoys the security of behavior patterns and established guidelines. This is one of the reasons dogs take to obedience training and like to learn tricks.

Coprophagy (Stool Eating)

Although coprophagy is distasteful in appearance, it is not harmful to the dog except for the control of intestinal parasites. The exact cause isn't known, but experts agree that it's a mental or dietary deficiency, or both.

I've noticed in many cases of parasitism that the dog gets a perverted appetite, eating feces, or possibly dirt, or he will chew on stones or other inedible objects. Another possible cause is a mineral or vitamin deficiency causing the dog to have a craving for something he's not getting in his normal diet.

In young puppies one of the commonest causes of stool eating is incomplete digestion of meat. Meat is passed in the feces in the same condition as before ingestion. This is likely due to intestinal worms, too much meat at one meal, or too large chunks. Sometimes cooking the meat for the puppy will cure this habit.

A new theory attributes coprophagy to an enzyme deficiency which can be corrected by the feeding of glandular organs (e.g., heart muscle) and by the use of enzymes in the daily diet.

Once a physical abnormality is ruled out, I would apply pressure on the dog regarding this habit. It is seen in young puppies more often than in adult dogs, and I approve of punishment for ridding the dog of the habit.

Many people have tried to discourage the habit by making the stools distasteful to the dog by the addition of various preparations. For example, a commercial drug called Ectoral which is used to kill fleas and ticks seems to give the stools an offensive taste. Other substances, helpful in some cases, are monosodium glutamate (sold commercially as "Accent"), oil of anise, and papain (an enzyme used in meat tenderizers). Any of these added to the dog's food should make the stool undesirable.

Extroversion

This classifies the dog who makes friends with everybody and is in love with the whole world.

Hallucinations

Under stress some dogs will snap at and chase imaginary objects, such as flies which aren't there.

Hysteria

Hysteria is not uncommon in nervous dogs. A prime example is dogs who are afraid of storms. I've known some on a hysterical binge to practically take a house apart during a storm. Such a dog begins pacing and panting well in advance of the storm. When he gets uncontrollable, it's impossible to calm him; he snaps and bites at everything. The treatment is to slip him a "Mickey Finn" at the first sign of an impending storm—a tranquilizer or a sedative.

For some nervous dogs just the threat of a bath, a pill to be taken, or toenails to be trimmed is enough to make them hysterical. Such high-strung dogs often chew at themselves, causing lesions on their bodies which we classify as neuro-dermatitis.

Mass hysteria can be precipitated in a group of dogs quite easily. All it takes is one dog to get overexcited and hysterical, and they all lose control of themselves. Unfortunately they often pick on one poor defenseless dog and mutilate him.

Introversion

This is the opposite of extroversion. These dogs stay close to home and will have nothing to do with strangers.

Phobias

A phobia is an abnormal fear of someone or something which is the result of a conditioned learning reflex. Dogs develop certain phobias for individuals and events which can start in a small way and build up to a hysterical condition. A good example is a phobia to the postman or to garbagemen.

Some dogs have an abnormal fear of the veterinary hospital—but not any more abnormal than some people's fear of a dental appointment.

Sexual Abnormalities

Sexual abnormalities are common in dogs of all ages and both sexes.

The female will mount other dogs, male or female, and even children, in the manner of the male and try to perform the sex act. If the bitch is in season, this is not abnormal, but some females show more or less constant signs of heat every 3 or 4 months instead of every 6 months. This is due to cystic ovaries which produce excessive female hormones. The condition might be counteracted by the injection of hormones, and if not, a hysterectomy is indicated, as these bitches are difficult to breed.

Male dogs will also perform this riding of legs and will even mount a child who is crawling on the floor. This is not uncommon during the normal breeding season, but some dogs who are confined and not allowed to roam develop the habit from sexual frustration. It can become intolerable, and dangerous to children. We use female hormones to try to counteract the condition, and if not successful, and it's impossible to breed the dog, castration is indicated.

Homosexual masturbation is common in the canine kingdom. Males ride males, and females ride females. The pleasure is derived from the clitoris or the penis rubbing against the body of the other animal. The female receives a clitoridean orgasm when she rides another female, and by her reactions it is obvious that she enjoys the sexual act. The male may even penetrate the anus of the other male dog.

The male dog also masturbates by having intercourse with such objects as towels, shoes, and stockings. He will also lick his penis until he has an erection and subsequent ejaculation. This dog when confronted with a female in season may or may not show any interest.

Pseudohermaphrodites are dogs having both male and female sex organs, and with such abnormal sexual features and hormonal imbalances their behavior is distinctly abnormal.

In one female dog whose sexual organs appeared normal, I found signs of a penis inside the vagina. This male organ would enlarge upon stimulation. The dog would allow herself to be mounted or would mount a female and attempt to copulate, depending on her mood or the stage of her irregular estrus cycle. She attracted male dogs but would not let them penetrate her.

There are male dogs that attract other males because of secondary female characteristics. They show signs of large nipple formation and a pendulous soft scrotum with abnormally soft testicles. The sheath of the penis is large and flabby. The testicles secrete a female hormone which affects the dogs both physically and mentally, and usually causes a chronic skin disorder.

For the physical and mental well-being of these dogs surgical intervention is recommended.

Temper Tantrums

Dogs display tantrums just like spoiled children and often are just as temperamental. They have emotional ups and downs much like their masters, whom they are trying to imitate. Sometimes it's difficult for the owner to recognize an outright case of temper tantrum, and he may attribute the abnormal behavior to other causes. When a mature dog chews furniture, rugs, and clothing, tears up curtains and draperies, and destroys other property in the house, he is having an unadulterated temper tantrum. Often the owner rationalizes the behavior by saying that the dog is difficult to train or isn't intelligent. This is seldom so; usually the dog is downright angry at being left alone.

By inadvertently leaving his television set on one time when he went out, a friend of mine found the answer to his dog's destructive tendencies when left alone. The dog had obviously become so engrossed in a program that he hadn't gotten around to destroying anything by the time my friend got home. It turned out the dog was perfectly content to be left alone watching TV. For some dogs, leaving a radio on will help.

If the problem isn't this easily solved, the dog should be punished immediately after the act is performed. If necessary, go out and when he thinks he's alone sneak in the back door and catch him in the act. Impress his wrongdoing upon him very sternly.

If you have a dog who is rebellious and won't respond to punishment, confine him to areas of the house where there's nothing that can be destroyed.

NEUROTIC ROLES

The Vicious or Aggressive Dog

Dogs aren't born vicious unless they're mentally unbalanced. The vicious dog isn't necessarily a nervous or neurotic dog, usually his viciousness is a product of his early environment, just as bad dispositions are more often the result of early environment than heredity. Viciousness per se is rare; animal acts of violence are rare. It is not inborn for a dog to fight without provocation—to fight unless for his life, his mate, his young, his possessions, or his human family. Even German shepherds and Dobermans trained for guard duty or armed forces service have to be taught to attack, and some of them can't be induced to bite, regardless of training.

When dogs run in packs, they revert to the call of the wild and become vicious. Keep your dog from joining a pack. With security in numbers, dogs have much more bravado and will attack other animals and even people. They should be considered dangerous.

A sudden rash of dog fights may mean a bitch in heat or approaching bad weather. Dogs, like people, take to fighting when the barometric pressure is falling.

Some dogs are downright bullies. They bully other dogs in the neighborhood and at times will try to scare and push people around too. This comes from primitive times when their instinct would have been to become leader. There are usually several dog fights in the neighborhood before a leader is established. Sometimes the other fellow feels that he still should be leader, and the fighting goes on. For certain male dogs who fight constantly, I recommend castration; it takes away some of their aggressiveness.

The male is generally larger and stronger and usually more aggressive, owing in part to the stimulus of male hormones. Females given male hormones will begin fighting, and males who are castrated will become more peaceful and try to avoid fights. Male dogs seldom will attack female dogs, but there are exceptions; there are some quite ungentlemanly males. But the aggressive tendency in females is serious because spaying will not relieve it. Some females are vicious with other females. The only suggestion I have is confinement, or a muzzle when you let the female out. Muzzling somewhat slows up aggressiveness because of the obvious handicap in a fight.

Breaking Up a Dog Fight. When trying to part two fighting dogs, be extremely careful. Even though your dog loves you, in the heat of battle he may bite you severely. It is best to try to pull him off either by his tail or by a rear leg; or if there's a broomstick or a pail of cold water handy, that may dampen the battlers' enthusiasm. Never, never put your hands near their heads or mouths.

The Tramp Dog

There are four main reasons why dogs run away from home:
(1) The call of the wild—the search for a mate. (2) Boredom.
There's not enough excitement or companionship at home. (3)
Unhappiness. The dog doesn't feel wanted by his human family
and will go elsewhere to find people who appreciate him more
fully. Sometimes jealousy is an underlying factor. (4) Love for
children. Dogs will seek out children because children usually
will take more time to play with them than adults.

The tramp dog leaves home at the slightest provocation, and
teams up with other dogs to become one of the pack, even
for a few days. If his reason for wandering is sexual, or if he
hears the call of the wild at certain times of the year, this can
be quite normal. And the dog who leaves the house in the
morning when everyone goes to work and school and then
returns at the hour of their return is quite normally bored at
being around the house by himself and goes out to seek adventure and playmates.

But there are neurotic dogs who are habitual wanderers.
They will stay away from home for days at a stretch. Usually
they leave home because they're lonely and are seeking the companionship of other dogs and humans.

In curing this habit you have to counteract the cause. If the
dog is lonesome at home, you have to provide more companionship. You have to show him he's loved and wanted. Just feeding
him plenty of his favorite food won't keep him at home. In
trying to correct a wandering dog, when he finally does return
from a prolonged trip, don't punish him when he first comes
to you; this will make him wander even more. He'll associate
returning home with punishment, and his trips will be longer
and longer. Treat him rather coolly. Then, after a few hours,
he'll come to you. That is when you start giving him lots of
affection, and some of his favorite food, to make him recognize
the love he's missing when wandering.

Of course, during breeding season the sexual urge is strong.
But there are some dogs who wander in search of females the

year round. For these dogs I advise castration; it will incline them to stay home. Attitudes change, and without the sexual motive as their main concern in life, the dogs become wholly concerned with their human families.

The Chaser

Some dogs seem to have a compulsion to run after small children—barking at them but not biting or even intending to bite. Occasionally the child falls and hurts himself and is scared half to death. The more the child screams and the faster he runs, the more persistent the dog is in the chase.

The performance of your dog is your responsibility. You are legally subject to arrest and conviction for owning a dog who is a public nuisance. You must attempt to stop his habit at once.

Here, too, you must catch the dog at the beginning of the tendency. It's best for the young puppy to grow up with children so that they become fast friends. At the slightest suggestion of his chasing a child, even though the puppy is only 3 or 4 months old, he must be punished. Be strict with your dog. Keep close supervision over him. Don't allow him to run free. In training him not to run after children, take him out on a rope 30 to 50 feet long, and when he attempts to go after a child, jerk him back strongly so that it pulls him off his feet. You have to reprimand him sternly and punish him severely. Then you have to supervise the dog closely as children play with him, until he loses his desire to chase them.

Other Animals. The three commonest objects of a dog chase are poultry, sheep, and cats. This is a serious problem because once a dog is accustomed to killing other animals and gets the "taste of blood," it's difficult to rehabilitate him. To him it's rare sport. He doesn't kill animals for food but rather for the thrill of the chase. He loves to see them run from him and to show his speed and dexterity with the subsequent kill.

Your dog is your personal property, and thus you are responsible for any damage that he may do, to either property or people.

If you intend to raise a puppy in the country where there are chickens or sheep, begin at an early age to get him used to walking among the poultry and animals. You should be with him at all times during his indoctrination period.

I've seen dogs chase horses and cows, and seen them receive a sharp hoof to the body or head while trying to nip at legs. I've seen large German shepherds kill young colts, and I've seen them kill calves. At this age it's difficult to rid them of the habit. I'd muzzle them or move them to the city.

There are many methods for curing the bloodthirsty habit. One method of curing a dog of chicken killing is to whip him over the head with the slain chicken and then tie the dead chicken around his neck until it practically rots off.

Another method is the use of a BB gun. When the animal walks among the chickens (or sheep) and gives the slightest growl or indication of viciousness, he receives a BB shot in his hide. Usually the owner is out of sight, and the animal doesn't know where the shot is from. However, he soon associates pain with his aggressive act.

Many dogs love to chase cats. If the cat would stand its ground, hiss and become ferocious, most dogs would stop short and think twice about attacking those sharp teeth and raking claws. In the main, tomcats and Siamese cats are a match for any dog and can handle themselves in any fight.

Your treatment should be about the same as with poultry and sheep. Severely punish your dog if he shows any tendency to chase cats. Of course, the best prevention is to have your puppy grow up with a kitten; they'll become the best of friends. Unfortunately, once a dog has the feeling for chasing and killing cats, the habit tends to persist.

Cars. Chasing cars is a sporting event for dogs, as it takes them back to primitive times when they chased game for their food. Nowadays chasing the big things on wheels is a substitute for the food-finding instinct. Also, it is possible that some of the dogs are trying to protect their neighborhoods from the monsters and that others, like the collie, are trying to herd them. Some breeds are worse offenders than others, and without a doubt the collie dog is the worst, but any breed is susceptible to the lure of the chase.

Most dogs are smart enough when chasing a car to stay right at the side of it, snapping and barking at the tires. However, occasionally there's a mishap and a good dog is killed. Numerous accidents have occurred because some motorists try to swerve or stop suddenly, with bad results to the human beings involved.

It's a habit that should be stopped if at all possible, but it's not an easy one to deal with. I've treated some dogs three and four times for being run over by an automobile. But the victims, as soon as the casts are off their legs, instead of being scared of cars, are off to the races again. Some dogs can be cured of the habit if the trainer is strict enough. There are several methods.

The most widely used method is to have a stranger in a strange car (dogs will not chase the cars in their family) drive by with a water pistol loaded with ammonia water (1 tsp. of household ammonia to a pint of water). The liquid is squirted into the dog's eyes and face as he approaches the car. This has to be repeated several times. The ammonia solution is strong enough to impress the dog with pain when he chases the car, but not strong enough to damage his eyes.

Another method is to get a friend who is a stranger to the dog drive by with a whip. As the dog approaches the car, he has to let him have it. Several sharp blows to the body should impress on him that there is pain associated with chasing cars.

A third method is to tie a piece of wood—a two-by-four—or an empty gallon tin can to the dog's neck so that when he attempts to run he trips over the wood or can. All these methods have to be repeated often until embedded in his mind.

The Biter

The biter is usually an animal who is aggressive. Some of these dogs are quite neurotic, and anything that moves in front of them—motorcycle, bicycle, running child—they will go after. It's almost like a game to them—like attacking an enemy. As the dog usually has his reasons for biting, we should attempt to get at the root of the problem and try to correct it. In most communities a dog is allowed three bites and after the third one is condemned to death.

The bad habit is sometimes brought about by excessive roughness when playing as a puppy. Some people do play too roughly with their puppies—teasing them with their hands and feet. As the dog gets older—his teeth larger and his jaws stronger—this play becomes more dangerous.

Biting should be corrected in the early stages before it's deeply ingrained in the dog's mind. Obedience training is helpful in that the dog will learn to follow your commands. The punishment for biting should be a sharp slap across the muzzle to show him that his mouth and the biting are what you are displeased with. Use either a newspaper or a leather strap, depending on the severity of the bite. Biting is a reprehensible habit and should be dealt with promptly and sternly.

Castration will slow down extremely aggressive male dogs. Although their motives for biting may not be entirely sexual, the operation takes away some of their male aggressiveness and they calm down to a walk. But castration will not help the neurotic dog who bites because he's panicky.

It is sometimes necessary to resort to a muzzle when turning the biting dog loose in the neighborhood. There are cities and towns where muzzling the at-large dog is required by law. I don't believe that muzzling is cruel to a dog. There are comfortable muzzles on the market; and sometimes a dog can be kept in the neighborhood who otherwise would have to be sent away or put to sleep.

Occasionally we get a dog who is incorrigible and can be classified as a canine criminal. No amount of training will correct his biting. If he's a large dog, such as a German shepherd or a Doberman, I advise military service if possible. Such dogs might also be used for guard duty in certain organizations. I certainly don't advise them as home pets; they're untrustworthy and the danger to children in the neighborhood is too great to take chances. These animals should either be given away to places in the country or, in some drastic cases, be put to sleep.

With the millions of dogs in the United States, there is the occasional criminal act of a dog attacking a human being. In my opinion this dog has flipped his lid—has become mentally unbalanced. If he were being defended in court, his attorney would plead that his act was committed during a fit of insanity. There is the age-old expression that the barking dog never bites. This is not so. If a dog is growling or barking at you, don't run from him. Stand your ground, and more often than not he'll leave you. If you run from him, he'll likely take after you and attack.

The Barker

There are many neurotic dogs who love to bark; they're enchanted with the sound of their own voices. The neurotic apartment-type dog barks from loneliness and boredom. He craves attention and wants everyone to know he's there. Every time he hears someone in the hall, or sees someone outside the window, he barks to let the world know that he's a member of the family and also its protector. Every dog has the protective instinct of the guard dog, even if he's not trained for it.

The worst offender is the night barker. This dog usually has slept all day and is coming alive when the master is ready for bed. Sometimes a hard run before retiring will get the dog too exhausted to bark. As for the other barkers, since dogs bark because they're lonely and crave companionship, spend as much time as possible with your pet when you're home. Needless to say, the barking habit is best corrected in the puppy before it becomes embedded. Here again sternness and consistency are required. If your dog barks only when you're away, sneak back to catch him at it and punish him so he'll be able to associate his barking with disapproval. There are comfortable muzzles which you can put on your dog to prevent him from barking. Muzzling is not a cure, but is an answer when it is imperative that he be quiet. Sometimes a dog will associate the muzzle with punishment for his barking and will be cured.

Female hormones given to adult male dogs eventually reduce or even suppress excessive barking. The female hormones
suppress the male hormones and reduce the aggressive and
territorial-defense barking. If the male is not desirable for
breeding purposes, I recommend castration as a permanent cure;
it will quiet him down in many ways.

The Wetter or Dribbler

Most of these dogs are so neurotic and such a bundle of
nerves that they can't help wetting the floor. When you approach them, they wet the floor out of fear and apprehension.
Yelling at them makes matters worse, and they wet even more.

In primitive days when an older dog pushed a younger
dog around, the younger dog would usually wet as a sign of
submission. He was plain scared of the larger and older animal.

It's not an easy neuroticism to correct. The dog has to first
believe that you're not attempting to hurt him when you approach him. You have to fill this dog with kindness—be gentle
and tender with him; bring him along slowly.

Of course, not all wetting is neurotic per se. There are some
dogs who show such behavior out of pure orneriness or stub-
bornness; and some of it can be considered abnormal. They are
completely housebroken dogs who wet curtains, floor, and furniture just to get even with their masters. Some male dogs wet
the house and one another as part of the territorial instinct—
to mark off their property.

Before you severely punish one of these dogs, you should
have him examined for a kidney problem. With certain kidney
diseases the dog can't control his urine. In older dogs prostatitis
is common, and it gives the dog an uncontrollable urge to
urinate often.

The House Nuisance

This is the neurotic dog who either has been neglected in
training or has been allowed too much of his own way around
the house. He's usually everywhere and in everyone's hair. He

carries his food from room to room, sleeps where he pleases, takes over the best furniture and loves to lie in doorways. He jumps up on your guests with his dirty paws, and when they sit down he jumps into their laps and licks their faces. He is the dog who sits under the dining-room table at mealtime begging for food.

It is difficult to punish these sweet brats, but most of us have friends who find such behavior reprehensible. Should you have such a dog and decide to take things in hand, if he's out of puppyhood a lot of the dies have been cast, and stern and consistent discipline is the only cure.

A tip on jumping up on people: As the dog jumps up to you bring your knee up to meet his chest or chin. Several such clips with your knee should discourage the habit. Or step on his hind toes as he jumps. Usually light pressure will suffice.

In scolding him for jumping onto Aunt Phoebe's needlepoint chair, I suggest you hit him lightly with a rolled-up newspaper or a bit of strap to make him associate the punishment with the crime. Then leave the disciplinary object in the chair; that will add emphasis and accessibility.

The Digger

In digging, dogs are reverting to primitive instincts; they're looking for a gopher or other hunted game, making themselves a place where they can lie down in the cool ground, burying a bone. Often they pick a spot near your favorite shrubbery.

It's a difficult habit to cure. Punishment at the scene of the crime may help in time. You have to wait until you catch the culprit in the act of digging. Then you can shout at him to stop and throw objects, such as tin cans, to scare him. If he leaves the scene of the crime, catch him by the collar and haul him back to the hole, reprimanding him by calling him "bad dog" and other well chosen words. At the same time give him a good shaking by the collar. Repeating this a time or two should cure him. Another method is to clip nails very close so digging hurts dog's paws.

The Timid-Shy Dog

A timid-shy dog is not necessarily a coward. He lacks confidence in himself because of a traumatic experience in puppyhood. The cowardly type will fight only in packs. If he's alone and sees another dog coming, he'll put his tail between his legs and go off. The cowardly dog is not necessarily a neurotic dog; the timid-shy dog usually is.

If the timid-shy dog isn't properly rehabilitated, he will be forever retiring and shy. You can't rush at him or approach him quickly, for in his fear he might bite you. In rehabilitating him, it takes patience and tender loving care to renew his confidence in you and the human race. In the female, if the shyness is not inherited, breeding her will sometimes help. Raising puppies may give her confidence.

Where the shyness is inherited it's doubtful whether you can train the dog to be an outgoing personality. You should teach him in a quiet voice with lots of praise and patting. Never make a sudden movement. Obedience training works well on these dogs if done gently.

The Runt of the Litter. Litter mates, sometimes with the aid of their mother, will combine to persecute one individual in the litter. This usually occurs between the 9th and 10th weeks. Whenever the persecuted puppy tries to get back into the nest, the others continually harass it. This puppy will be timid-shy and undernourished, but can be rehabilitated.

The Overdependent Dog

The overdependent dog is the one who is reared as a perpetual puppy. There's a close emotional bond between this pet and its owner, and any disturbance in the daily routine will send the dog into a hysterical state.

The cause can be visitors, the absence of the owner from the house, or a visit to the veterinarian or boarding kennel. When they're severely disturbed, such dogs when left alone in a house over a long period may become destructive. Usually a babysitter is in order. If not a human babysitter, you might get another puppy or a kitten; even a TV set may help the dog's anxiety and depression. Such animals are good subjects for tranquilizers.

The Dope Fiend

There are some dogs who get hooked on certain narcotics or sedatives. They become dependent both on the drugs and on the attention they receive.

One of my patients became so used to getting phenobarbital for his twitching body (chorea, as a sequela to distemper) that every night at ten o'clock he sat up and begged for his pill. He wouldn't go to sleep without it. Finally, after months of barbiturates, we changed the pill to aspirin and he was completely satisfied—slept like a baby.

HOW TO HELP THE NEUROTIC DOG

Dogs respond to proper treatment, and it's up to each of us to find the proper way for his dog.

To fight excessive nervousness in a dog here are some good rules to follow:

—Don't give him many commands at once. Go slowly.

—Don't teach him more than he can comprehend in a 10- to 20-minute session.

—Be firm with him and make him understand that when you tell him to do something, he must do it or be punished.

—Give him plenty of companionship.

—Give him plenty of play and exercise.

—Allow him to be in the company of many strangers, preferably the children in the neighborhood. Most dogs are gentle with children.

TRANQUILIZERS

Tranquilizers play an important role in veterinary medicine and especially in handling and quieting nervous and neurotic dogs. But drugs are potent and should not be used without the advice of a professional.

Tranquilizers are useful in calming dogs fearful of storms, cars, firecrackers, and guns. They are helpful with the bitch undergoing false pregnancy, to overcome her anxiety over the missing puppies; with the shy bitch, to overcome her fears of the male during mating; with the nervous bitch, when she is whelping and to overcome the possibility of refusal to nurse her puppies; and with the bitch who has been known to kill her puppies. They are useful in the control of itching skin, in some coughs caused by irritation, in asthma, and in vomiting. They are helpful when training animals, to overcome their neuroses. They calm the animal down to the point where he will listen to the owner or trainer. They are also used by veterinarians for minor operations, such as surgery, eye treatment, teeth cleaning, and even grooming and clipping. And they are helpful to kennel owners when nervous pets are boarding at the kennel—barkers, finicky eaters, etcetera.

But tranquilizers are not a permanent cure for any neuroses. They are just in-between treatment until proper training and rehabilitation can be initiated. The causes of the neuroses should be delved for and dug out.

With the vicious dog, tranquilizers should be used with care and not be depended on entirely. Even in a moment, if the tranquilizer doesn't sedate the dog, or before it takes effect, he may perform a criminal act and hurt a child or a dog. Sometimes instead of helping him, the tranquilizer seems to mix him up even more, and he becomes more unstable and more difficult to handle.

BRAIN SURGERY FOR THE VICIOUS DOG

Many guard dogs returning from war duty and other vicious dogs that need rehabilitation have been helped by brain surgery. A prefrontal lobotomy, similar to that performed in human beings, has given consistently good results. The animal becomes timid and within a few weeks develops a desirable personality.

5 PUPPY CARE AND TRAINING

The formula for raising a healthy puppy is to start him off right and follow through with a good management program, which should involve the following factors: (1) proper housing; (2) proper sanitation; (3) proper nutrition; (4) control of parasites and disease; (5) proper training.

Before taking a puppy home, you should receive all necessary information about past wormings and vaccinations. Get the name of the serum or vaccine that the puppy has received so that there will be no misunderstanding. Many puppies have become victims of distemper because their owners thought that when the puppy was vaccinated at the age of 6 weeks, he received immunization for life. Likewise, some people assume that if a puppy is wormed at 6 weeks, another worm checkup will not be necessary for a year or two.

The first 6 months of a puppy's life is the most dangerous period, as he is susceptible to anything and everything, and especially to diseases and parasites. I advise the new owner to take the puppy to a veterinarian within a day or two for a thorough checkup. If there is anything wrong—for example, a congenital defect or a disease—the puppy can usually be returned, with some form of remuneration. But most important, the good health of the puppy will be ensured, and a schedule will be set up for future vaccinations and wormings.

INTRODUCTION TO THE NEW HOME

The puppy will be lonesome for the companionship of his brothers and sisters and for the warmth of his mother's breast. He will want to be cuddled. He must be treated gently, and with a minimum of noise and confusion, as he gradually becomes acquainted with his new family. He is all yours, and you are all that he has. As a dog is man's best friend, so also is man a dog's best friend.

If possible, bring the puppy home early in the day so that by nighttime he will have checked out the house. When he first arrives, he should be given some warm milk, and then light and frequent feedings. A prime mistake of new dog owners is to put down a large bowl of food and let the puppy eat all he wants. Most puppies will gorge themselves right into extreme digestive disturbances. After being made to feel secure in his oral needs, and about where he is to eat, the puppy should be shown where he will sleep, where he will exercise and where he will eliminate. He should of course, be confined to parts of the house not easily soiled.

The first 10 days are the most difficult, and since the dog is a creature of habit, he must be run on a fairly rigid schedule. He wants to be taught, and his lessons should be repeated until he gets the point.

However, no advice that I can give, or that you read elsewhere, should be hard and fast, but should be something worked out between your dog and your family. As no two dogs and no two people are alike, you will have to adjust what you read to you and your dog.

The Bed

It is wise to give the puppy a bed of his own. It gives him a sense of ownership. For an overly boisterous or destructive puppy, a shipping crate can be used. As well as serving as a bed, it will keep him confined, and as most puppies will not soil their beds, it will help in housebreaking too.

The first night or so puppies tend to be homesick but will usually settle down if taken to bed with one of the family. Unless this is to be allowed every night, however, it should be done only as a last resort; the puppy will substitute the family member for his mother and will expect a human bed the rest of his life.

Some puppies will be content in their own bed with a hot-water bottle to cuddle, or a ticking clock, or an old shoe. In severe cases a baby aspirin or a wee bit of a sleeping pill will quiet the puppy and allow everyone a good night's sleep.

HOUSEBREAKING

Most puppies are a bit nervous at first and are liable to have an accident or two. Don't be upset; be gentle and patient. In housebreaking it is up to the owner to instruct, not to condemn. Teach the puppy properly, and he will respond graciously. Don't punish him unless you are sure that you are communicating with him—that he understands what you are trying to convey to him. The dog is the closest of all animals in communication with humans; he will understand if you are explicit enough.

The average dog takes 4 to 6 weeks for complete housebreaking, but there are problem dogs and problem cases. Patience, understanding, and a ready mop are requisites. The muscles which control the bladder and intestines develop with age. Give the puppy a chance—it takes time. Success in housebreaking depends on whether you, the dog owner, can be trained. Any failure in housebreaking is usually the owner's fault.

Age to Start

Even though progress is slower with puppies under several months of age, it is never too early to start. Housebreaking may take several weeks with a puppy acquired at 6 weeks of age. Less time is required for one at 3 months. And only a few days are needed for a puppy 6 months old. Don't expect too much before 12 weeks of age; but the earlier you start, the quicker the puppy will respond.

Responsibility

Although various members of the household may help, it is best for one person to be responsible for most of the training; otherwise everyone's job soon becomes no one's job.

Supervision

Housebreaking is not a part-time task; constant supervision is necessary. The puppy must be aired upon rising, once or twice after each meal, as often as possible during the day, and especially after playing and before retiring. Dogs usually prefer to eliminate outside, and the puppy must be kept out until he has completely relieved himself. He should be praised; and if he is given a tidbit each time, the association will soon make him eliminate quickly to get his reward.

Prevention

In forming habits, an ounce of prevention is worth many pounds of correction. Watch the puppy closely. An expectant look, running back and forth to the door, and scratching at it will all indicate his needs. This is the time to get him outdoors at once. Each accident inside prolongs the housebreaking process, both by breaking down the correct habit and by providing the puppy with a place inside that he will have a tendency to use.

Regularity

Feed the puppy on a regular schedule and take careful note of his habits. Bowel movements usually occur a short time after eating. Exercise the puppy after each meal and try to get him to eliminate before allowing him back inside the house. Take him to the same area over the same route; he has a strong association for previous odors. Try to take him out at regular intervals that he can rely on, and he will soon get into the swing of things.

Some puppies stay cleaner at night if fed lightly toward evening and not fed at all after about 8 P.M. Other puppies require a feeding right before bedtime—11 to 12 P.M.—in order to stay quiet during the night. The time for the last feeding can be experimented with, earlier or later, depending on the puppy's digestive system and his ability to contain his bowel movements until morning.

Confinement

Don't allow a puppy the complete run of the house and expect him to find his way to the door each time he has to eliminate. In the daytime he should be confined to a small area where there is a linoleum surface, such as the kitchen or utility room. At night he should be confined to a small area which is well covered with newspapers. As most dogs will not soil their bedding, an older puppy who persists in having a bowel movement during the night could be confined to a small sleeping box.

Discipline

The memory of the puppy is about 30 seconds long; if he is disciplined after that time, he will not realize what he has done wrong. Try to act as quickly as possible when he errs. Either catch him in the act or take him back to the bad deed and discipline him at the spot. As soon as he has been disciplined, he should be rushed outside to the area which he is to use for elimination.

Usually scolding is adequate to show the puppy the extent to which he has fallen into disfavor. He will want to avoid such scenes. Some puppies' feelings are badly hurt at being shamed. But too, most dogs love to be praised. Be lavish with praise and petting when indicated. If scolding doesn't work, most puppies will respond to the sound of a newspaper being slapped against a hand or the floor. Persistent offenders (assuming you are not at fault) may require spanking with a rolled-up newspaper.

Paper Training

Training to newspapers may be the wisest procedure in cold weather or for people who live in apartments. Several thicknesses of newspapers are spread out on the floor, preferably on tile or linoleum. All the principles of training described above are employed except that the puppy is placed on the papers instead of outside. It is surprising how soon the puppy will want to feel the newspapers under him before eliminating. Since dogs tend to return to their own odors, some people keep one soiled newspaper to entice the puppy to the same spot. Once he knows what the papers are for, he can be taken outside on papers until he gets the idea that he is to go outside, then the papers can be discarded. Be sure to scrub immediately all mistakes with a disinfectant and deodorant (such as chlorox, pine oil or lysol) to remove odors so that the pup will not return to the scene of the crime again.

There are some excellent commercial aids for training puppies to newspapers. They have the odor of urine, which draws the puppy to the spot. Although they are helpful, they are not the total answer.

Problem Dogs

There are some problem dogs who never seem to be housebroken. In reality the dog eventually housebreaks his owner so that the owner will take him out at regular intervals.

Some spoiled dogs refuse to be housebroken, in order to punish their owners.

For certain problem dogs the discipline has to involve a certain amount of physical pain, but it should never be severe.

There are some dogs who cannot be housebroken, but not because they don't want to be. Sometimes a puppy cannot control his bladder or bowels. A veterinarian should check to make sure that infection or parasites are not causing the incontinence.

Sometimes it helps to take the puppy out with older dogs, and through imitation he learns that he is to relieve himself outdoors.

When a puppy doesn't seem to be able to get the idea of housebreaking, it is best to confine him to the kitchen as much as possible and to leave his leash on him all the time. In this way you can immediately give him a slight tug at the collar, accentuated with a firm "No!" He will soon learn that each time he makes a mistake there will be a tug and a harsh word. Take him outdoors immediately, and when he eliminates praise him as if he had performed a marvelous deed.

Some General Facts About Housebreaking

During the first 2 to 3 weeks puppies urinate and defecate in response to licking by the mother. After 3 weeks they leave the nest to urinate and defecate. By 8 to 9 weeks they localize the functions in definite spots. Normally a puppy 8 to 12 weeks of age is expected to have a call of nature every 2 hours.

Clean up the mistake carefully and take the cloth with the odor on it outdoors to the spot designated for elimination. In this way you convey to the puppy what is wanted of him. Incidentally, when puppies urinate on rugs, wash the spot out with soap and water, and then club soda, which is an excellent detergent for urine spots. A turkish towel pressed to the spot for a few hours will dry it out.

In housebreaking, don't just put a puppy out; take him out, otherwise he'll forget why he's out, and you won't know if he actually performed. Cold rain or snow shouldn't stop either of you. The puppy has a thick enough coat to be insulated against the weather.

There are some dogs who in the beginning will not relieve themselves well on a lead and have to be turned loose. This modesty should be overcome if one lives where it is dangerous to allow a dog to run. It is better for him to be constipated until he is broken from such a habit than to be killed.

As a rule females are housebroken more easily. They relieve themselves more modestly and require less shrubbery and trees than males. The male is more anxious to roam—looking for adventure and sex.

To sum it all up, feeding on schedule, regular walks, and instant scolding will quickly housebreak a puppy.

FEEDING THE PUPPY

During the first 90 days after weaning there is particularly rapid growth in the puppy and therefore the need for a high amount of protein. The extra protein enables the puppy to cope better with emergencies in his early life, such as diseases and parasites.

Proper nourishment will help the puppy's body to develop immunity against parasites, diseases, and serious infections which strike early in life.

All puppies vary in food requirements. What may be sufficient for one may be famine for another. A weaning puppy should be fed at least 5 or 6 times a day. For the 3-month-old puppy frequent feeding is advocated. From 10 weeks on he should be fed 4 meals a day, up to 4 months. Three meals daily between 4 and 6 months should be fed and 2 meals a day between 6 months and a year. After 1 year of age most dogs require only one meal a day. However, this is arbitrary. Each dog should be fed according to his needs; and the type of food and its quality must be considered in determining how many times a day to feed.

The following is a typical feeding schedule for a medium-sized breed—30 to 50 pounds at maturity. It can be altered to suit small breeds or extra-large breeds by drawing comparisons:

Age	*Weight*	*Feedings*
2 months	6-8 pounds	*Morning* 5-6 tbsp. milk 3-4 tbsp. cereal or dog food *Noon* 1-2 heaping tsp, daw ground meat or commercial canned or dry *Afernoon* Repeat morning feeding *Evening* Repeat noon feeding *Bedtime* (late evening): 5-6 tbsp. milk
3 months	10-15 pounds	Increase amounts per feeding according to puppy's growth and capacity. Gradually eliminate afternoon and bedtime feedings

4 months	15-25 pounds	*Morning* ½-1 cup milk 4-8 tbsp. cereal or dog food *Noon* 4-8 heaping tbsp. raw ground meat or commercial canned or dry food *Evening* 4-8 tbsp. meat or dog food 3-6 tbsp. cooked mashed vegetables or table scraps
6 months	25-30 pounds	*Morning* ¾-1½ cups milk ¾-1½ cups cereal or dog food *Noon* ½-1 cup meal or dog food mixed with ¼-1 cup cereal or dry dog food *Evening* 1-2 cups meat ½-1 cup dog food ½-1 cup vegetables or table scraps
8 months	about 30 pounds	*Morning* 1½ cups milk toast, cereal, dog food, or dry dog food *Evening* 2 cups meat cereal or toast vegetables or table scraps
9 months	30-40 pounds	*Morning* milk and cereal (2 cups each) *Evening* 2 cups meat 2 cups table scraps or dry dog food
10 months	40-50 pounds	*Morning* Milk or cereal or dog food if he will eat it. Some do not want the morning meal at this age *Evening* 3 cups meat or dog food and vegetables or table scraps

12 months	maturity	Total amount of food—1-1⅓ lbs. per day:
		1½ cups meat
		1½ cups cereal or dry dog food
		1½ cups vegetables or table scraps

The delicate digestive system of a puppy at weaning frequently requires a soft, bland diet before a regular adult ration can be tolerated. Baby cereals and baby foods are excellent.

A safe rule for frequency is "demand feeding." But don't give the puppy all he wants, as he is sure to be a glutton. Feed him all that he will digest without upsetting him. Some puppies double their weight in 2 to 3 weeks, so the quantity has to be adjusted accordingly.

The amount of food that a puppy demands depends somewhat on breed, amount of exercise, and general condition. A general rule, although arbitrary, is ½ ounce of food per pound of dog weight, per day. The dog should be fed at regular times so that he can count on and look forward to his meals.

Small breeds need more food per pound of body weight than do the large breeds. When they see a St. Bernard or a Great Dane, most people shudder to think of the food bills. But be assured that the giants eat extremely large amounts of food only during the first year or year and a half of their growth. After they have reached maturity, they don't eat much more than a collie or German shepherd. The owner of a St. Bernard or a Great Dane will feed more to his puppy the first year of his life than he will for the next 2 years.

Raw meat is more easily digested than cooked meat. Too much fat is not good for a puppy, although small amounts should be an integral part of the diet. The puppy can have most kinds of meat, such as beef, lamb, and chicken. Meat products such as liver, tripe, and kidney are beneficial additives. Horse meat is too strong for some puppies and gives them diarrhea. Egg yolks are excellent, raw or cooked, but the whites are not beneficial, especially raw.

Throughout the first year of his life the puppy should have daily amounts of vitamins and minerals added to his food. These can be in powder, liquid, or tablet form.

The health of the puppy depends on the kinds of meals that he is given every day. Fortunately the days of haphazard feeding are over. A good puppy chow prepared by a commercial company provides a basic well-balanced diet, and such a food should make up the major part of the dog's diet.

Supplements

Puppies need variety in food as well as we do, and table scraps and leftovers are an excellent means of breaking up the monotony of the everyday diet. But they should be used as a supplement and not as the main part of the diet.

Vegetables are fine for puppies and are a good food supplement. Potatoes are not injurious, as is widely believed, and within proportion are an excellent supplement. Cake, candy, and other sweets are all right to give a puppy, within reason. And incidentally, candy does not cause worms.

With their tender gums and growing teeth, most puppies enjoy gnawing on objects such as human flesh, expensive shoes, and antique furniture. The addition of kibbled food to the daily ration or the occasional large bone can provide distraction and fine therapy for teeth and gums. It should be a large beef bone, preferably a knuckle. Beef bones are all right if they are of the large variety, but rib bones or T-bones are often injurious, as they tend to break off in sharp points and cause damage to the intestinal tract. Never give small bones, such as chicken, pork, veal, lamb, or rabbit; they are injurious to throats and intestines.

Some people put chicken bones into the pressure cooker, which thoroughly softens them. Bones prepared in this way will not harm the dog, and the nutritional benefits are excellent.

Loss of Appetite

If a puppy refuses a feeding, take the food away and try again in an hour or two. If he refuses more than 2 or 3 meals, a veterinarian should be consulted, as this is a sure sign that something is wrong. A puppy must not go more than 8 hours without food; he will dehydrate, weaken, and go into shock very quickly.

Sometimes a puppy will be distracted and would rather play than eat. Keep eating and play periods separate.

Most puppies gulp their food and seldom chew it. This has nothing to do with manners and is perfectly normal. Often a puppy will regurgitate his food and then eat it again. Don't stop him from doing this no matter how distasteful it may seem to you. This is his way of predigesting his food, and is an ancestral instinct.

The Finicky Eater

There are some cuties who will hold out for filet mignon no matter what entree you put in front of them. And of course there are those who contend that the puppy will be spoiled if he is given steaks and chops and presumably will not eat commercial dog food. This may be so, but a combination of the two becomes a palatable mixture for a finicky eater.

For the finicky eater, the master must experiment and compromise. Often a puppy develops tastes which don't jibe with what the owner has in mind, and there is a constant battle of wits until either the puppy or the owner wins. A compromise is the best solution.

It may be necessary to change the diet frequently. Sometimes mix palatable table scraps with a commercial food in varying proportions. Or let the puppy miss a meal or two so that he will appreciate something he doesn't really care for (he thinks).

Overfeeding

Dogs are the most delightful beggars in the world. They love to plead for food. Don't be taken in and break down every time the dog begs. Overfeeding will result in diarrhea, vomiting, and a noisy intestinal tract.

It is not healthy for a puppy to get overweight; it puts a strain on his growing bones. It is much easier to keep his diet down than to reduce him.

Overfeeding a puppy to get a large-sized dog is not the way to do it. His size may be changed slightly—bulgingly—but heredity determines the final size of a dog and not the amount of food he is given.

Likewise, a toy-sized dog has to be bred from toy-sized parents and half-starving the dog will only make him sickly. Incidentally, the belief that feeding a puppy alcoholic beverages will stunt his growth, while widely held, has never been scientifically substantiated. (Fortunately, alcohol doesn't affect the growth rate of human creatures either.)

Don'ts

Don't allow a puppy to play or exercise strenuously immediately after eating. In some breeds, notably the Great Dane, the bloating can end in a ruptured stomach, which would be fatal.

Although a puppy should always have water handy, don't allow him to drink all he wants, especially after eating. Some puppies bloat up extensively.

Although milk is an excellent food, some puppies cannot properly assimilate it, and it gives them diarrhea. Buttermilk, however, is an excellent substitute for sweet milk and is desirable for puppies when they have a digestive upset. It restores the normal healthy bacteria to the intestinal tract during or after an illness, and it is an excellent additive during a siege of coccidiosis.

While a puppy is eating, it is best to leave him alone. And don't allow children near him. One of his ancestral instincts is to guard his food, and many a child has been bitten for getting too close to a feeding dog. Even the gentlest dog will defend his food.

Many a puppy has been poisoned by ingesting a foreign object. When you find the puppy eating something he's not supposed to, discipline him at once, and keep careful watch over him.

TEETHING

Beginning at the age of 4 months, the baby teeth (or milk teeth) fall out, allowing the adult teeth to push through the gums. By 7 to 8 months, if the baby teeth have not fallen out it is wise to have a veterinarian pull them. If they are left in, they can impede the permanent teeth and the puppy will be left with a double row of teeth or crooked teeth, which will hurt him cosmetically and in the show ring. The teeth should be taken out by a professional because if this is not done properly, they may break off at the roots and present complications in formation of the adult teeth.

Teething can cause the puppy to go off his feed, and there may be a slight diarrhea. The gums will be sore, and at such times a soft bland diet should be fed for a few days.

Most puppies like to chew on human flesh during the teething process, and it is judicious to teach them not to destroy too much of one's anatomy during this period.

TOYS

Hard-rubber toys, commercially prepared bones, and rawhide bones are fine for puppies to gnaw on, and they are soothing to sore gums and helpful in teething. Soft-rubber toys are taboo, as a puppy can quickly chew them up and the rubber that is swallowed can harm his intestinal tract.

Old neckties or several pairs of ladies' nylon hose tied together are safe and enjoyable for the puppy to play with. Toys amuse him and keep him from destroying the household.

GROOMING

Start the grooming program while the puppy is young and can be made to feel that grooming is a game. He will soon learn to look forward to being spruced up.

A soft brush is sufficient to keep most puppies in good condition. In a long-haired dog, a comb or wire brush will take care of the mats; and as he gets older a stiffer brush can be used.

In breeds that require trimming (Scotties, poodles, etc.) it is advisable to trim the heads and feet at an early age, for sanitary reasons and to get the puppy acclimated to the procedure. It must be done carefully and gently because if someone is rough during the first few trimmings, the puppy will become a problem dog and require tranquilizers for future trimmings.

It is a good idea to trim a puppy's nails also at an early age so that he will get used to it. Be careful about cutting them too close and making them bleed, since he will never forget the sharp pain. Try to make him believe that it is part of his play period—getting him to lie on his back or side. After the nails, the matted hair between toes and pads can also be cut. A puppy indoctrinated at an early age for this chore will be easy to cope with all his life. Some docile pets turn into tigers when someone attempts to trim their nails. This can usually be traced to an unhappy puppyhood experience.

Many people believe it is wrong to bathe a puppy under 6 months of age. This is not quite correct. In the summer a puppy can be bathed at an earlier age. But in cold weather one must keep the puppy from being exposed to cold and draft, as he is extremely susceptible to sore throats and colds. However, there are times when a puppy is so dirty that he needs a soap-and-water bath.

When a puppy is bathed for the first time, it must be done gently so as not to frighten him and make him forever afraid of water. Use cotton in each ear to keep out the water; and a little mineral oil or boric acid ointment in his eyes will avoid soap irritation. A mild baby soap or face soap should be used; strong flea soaps or harsh detergent soaps will dry the oils of skin and hair. After getting a good lather, rinse the puppy well, then dry him. After toweling a hair dryer can be used.

There are some excellent aerosol foam shampoos (dry shampoos) which produce suds that are lathered into the coat and skin without water. A towel is used to wipe off the excess suds. Although not quite so good as soap and water, the dry shampoos do take away a lot of dirt and can be used without worry during the winter months.

There are times when a sponge bath with a wet soapy cloth will do. Here again it should be a mild soap. Just rub the slightly damp cloth over the puppy's entire body and dry him thoroughly with towels.

For fleas or ticks, certain special puppy flea sprays and powders can be used. However, be careful of the strong flea dips used on adult dogs, as the puppy may absorb some through his skin or lick it, and it can prove fatal.

AILMENTS AND DISEASES

The commonest ailments of young puppies are vomiting and diarrhea. If a puppy vomits more than 2 or 3 times, one may well suspect that he has swallowed a foreign object. The puppy is curious by nature and will pick up and chew almost anything he comes upon. I have often had to surgically remove from puppies' stomachs or intestines such indigestible objects as golf balls, pins and needles, and razor blades, and on one occasion a diamond ring. A word of advice: if ever you are missing a small object and your puppy is vomiting, have his stomach X-rayed.

In a simple diarrhea, caused by overfeeding or teething, Kaopectate, Pepto-bismol, or bismuth (1 tsp. per 10 lbs. of puppy, 3 or 4 times a day) is soothing to the stomach and to the sensitive lining of the intestinal tract.

Intestinal parasites (worms), coccidiosis, or an infectious enteritis can be the cause of an intestinal upset, and if not treated in time can result in death.

Heavy infestation by fleas, lice, or ticks can produce anemia. Hookworms are especially serious; they suck the blood and lower the resistance to other diseases. There are efficient drugs for destroying hookworms in even very young puppies.

Coccidiosis is a disease which causes a chronic, insidious type of diarrhea. Severe cases show mucus and blood in the stools. The disease is increasing in frequency and is dangerous to the lives of puppies. Pet shops and kennels that don't practice proper sanitary procedures often spread it, as it is contagious from one puppy to another through contamination of the bowel movements.

Von Gierke syndrome, which is a condition in toy breeds, is

characterized by sudden coma, shock, and occasionally convulsions. Chihuahuas are mostly affected; Yorkshire terriers, Maltese terriers, and other small breeds also can be affected.

The cause is not completely known, although there seems to be a relationship in that stress conditions in young puppies cause hypoglycemia—a lowered level of sugar in the blood.

It can happen suddenly, without warning. The puppy is found in a semi-comatose condition with the usual signs of shock, such as pale gums and tongue, and dilated and unfocused eyes. The animal sometimes screams in pain.

Immediate attention is required to save the puppy. Karo syrup, molasses, or any other form of sugar should be poured slowly into the puppy's mouth. Stimulants, such as brandy, and warmth should be provided.

Any predisposing factor that causes lack of appetite, and no food for over 8 hours, can produce the syndrome (a puppy cannot go over 8 hours without food or water). Young toy puppies that are handled much or become exhausted are prone to this disorder. After an accident, illness, or any traumatic experience, force-feed the puppy with broth or eggnog.

Rickets is a condition of puppies caused by a deficiency of the minerals calcium and phosphorus. The minerals are helped in absorption by the presence of vitamins A and D.

Symptoms of rickets are bowed legs with large knots of bone at the leg joints. There are also knots of bone on the ribs. It is diagnostic to see a puppy with his toes spread in an awkward position and his legs bent at his carpal (wrist) joints.

Although any breed is susceptible to rickets, it is usually seen in fast-growing breeds, such as the Great Dane and German shepherd.

A deficiency of vitamins and minerals will also keep a puppy's ears from standing erect in such breeds as the boxer, Doberman, and Great Dane.

If a puppy does a lot of hiccupping, fear not. This is normal —spasms of the diaphragmatic muscle which occur at various times in the growing period. There is no pathological significance.

Signs of a Sick Puppy

—Vomiting
—Diarrhea
—Loss of appetite
—Lethargy, lassitude, listlessness
—Coughing
—Running eyes and nose
—High fever

Safety Rules for Puppies

—Give only large beef-knuckle bones
—Keep dangerous objects off the floor and out of reach
—Never, never worm a sick puppy
—Children should not be allowed to maul a young puppy
—Don't allow a puppy freedom of the outdoors if there is any danger from automobiles

EXERCISE, BEHAVIOR, TRAINING

Exercise

Overfeeding and insufficient exercise are the principal causes of fat, lazy, sluggish puppies; and this goes for adult dogs too. The dog's body is geared for running and playing, and both are necessary for his well-being. Lack of exercise can bring on all kinds of digestive disorders and physical and mental sluggishness. Playing with other dogs and humans provides physical and emotional gratification. A long walk with your puppy, besides being physically beneficial to both of you, is pleasing to his ego.

A puppy should be taken out every 2 hours, if possible, but at least 3 times a day. Walking with your dog should be a period of enjoyment as well as serious training for his future well-being. The earlier you leash-train him, the better. Teach him to walk a few steps in front of you, not constantly pulling on the leash.

I don't advise leashing or tying a puppy outdoors by him-self for a long time. He may become entangled in the leash or rope and injure himself. An outdoor pen or a fenced-in area is desirable so he can have some freedom on his own and be out-doors when the weather permits. Some shelter should be pro-vided in case of rain or on hot sunny days for shade. He should also have an ever-present pan of water. Some dogs prefer to be with humans and don't wish to stay outside by themselves. They should not be kept outside if they don't wish to stay, and certainly not in wet or cold weather especially if they are toy or small puppies.

Leash Training. A certain amount of psychology is needed in teaching the puppy to be towed along with a leash attached to his neck. Don't expect the puppy to walk along at your side the first time. Invariably he will fight and tug and pull.

The first step is to teach the puppy to wear a collar. Any time after 6 weeks of age a light collar can be put on him. He will not like it and will scratch at it and try to get it off but will soon resign himself to his fate.

Allow him to get used to the collar for a week or so, and then attach a short length of rope to the collar and let him play with it and drag it around the house. Occasionally pick up the rope and hold it so that he knows you have control of his collar. At first he will pull and tug and try to go in every direction. Don't jerk it, and he will soon realize that nothing drastic will happen to him when you hold the rope. He will get to like your playing with him—catching the rope.

The next step is to teach him to walk with you without get-ting under your feet. Repeat the lesson 2 or 3 times a day; just before mealtime is preferable because he will get a reward when it's over.

Behavior

There is an old saying, like master, like dog, and a diso-bedient or neurotic dog is often the result of poor training. There is a ring of truth to the statement that neurotic dogs are the result of neurotic owners. However, I don't wish to imply that all neurotic dogs have emotionally unstable owners.

Puppies are great imitators, and a shy or timid dog is often reflecting those tendencies of his owner. Also, it is well to choose a puppy's companions wisely. If there are any with bad faults, keep the puppy away as you would keep a child away from a juvenile delinquent.

Good kennel owners give their puppies daily individual care. It has been proved that dogs that are raised in isolation with no human contact develop emotional imbalances that interfere with normal development.

Infantile autism, commonly called kennelitis, is often seen in dogs left in kennels without human love. It is characterized by excessive shyness and introspection and is brought on more by environment than by heredity. Some of these dogs become fearful of everyone but their owners and develop fear-biting.

There is also a tendency for this to happen when a puppy receives too much love and affection from one person. The puppy becomes so attached to the person that he growls at or bites anyone else. Such puppies don't have enough contact with the outside world and distrust the human race.

I advise all dog owners to take their puppies with them on trips around town so that the puppies can see all shapes and sizes of human beings. It will show them that people are not out to harm them—that many people love dogs and will stop and compliment and pat them. A puppy should make friends with strangers, up to a point.

Most destructive dogs do their bad deeds out of boredom. They are not necessarily juvenile delinquents if they chew and destroy things. This is part of the development stage in normal, healthy puppies. Before leaving a puppy alone in the house, it is a good idea to take him for a long walk—tire him out—so he will nap while you are out. This also works well when taking a puppy on a car trip.

Training

Often I'm asked which breed is best for training. Although we see more poodles and German shepherds in obedience trials today, this doesn't necessarily mean that they are the smartest and most trainable. It just means that there are more of them. There is much convincing evidence that every breed is capable of doing well in obedience training, and that no one breed has a monopoly on brains. There are no "stupid" dogs. It is up to each owner to bring out his dog's inherent intelligence.

Each puppy is an individual in mentality and adaptability, and each master must supply the supervision that is needed to mold the development of the puppy's character and disposition. Some puppies are bold and some are shy, but the majority seem to be undecided which way they are going to develop.

Teaching the puppy his name is one of the first things to concentrate on. Pick a simple-sounding name and use it as much as possible every time you talk to him and with every command. He soon will learn that the word is his. When you call him and he comes to you, praise him, pat his head, and give him a tidbit. He should associate his name with something pleasant.

Start the training gently and tenderly and with much patience. Treat him as you would a child, with sympathy and understanding. Lavish upon him all the love that he deserves, and also the discipline that he deserves when he does wrong.

Don't be harsh with him. Yelling, cussing, kicking, and beating will not hurry up his training and more likely will deter him from the one and only desire in life, to please you, his loving master.

Don't expect miracles overnight. The puppy learns by repetition, and you must develop communication for complete and worthwhile training. Talk to him, explain to him and show him what you want. If he can't seem to learn something, teach him something else that he can do. He wants to learn, but we all have our limitations. Once you start teaching him something, keep repeating it until he understands completely.

The first rule in training is to make all lessons brief and interesting so that the puppy will not become bored.

In a training program rewards and discipline should be given immediately. Be lavish in your praise; it is important to the dog's ego to be complimented. Usually a disgusted voice is discipline enough. If something more forceful is needed, a rolled-up newspaper should be sufficient. Most dog trainers say the hand should never be used in punishment; and I certainly don't advise striking a dog on the head or backbone, as these are delicate areas. A light thump on the fanny or the sides will get the point across.

Dogs don't understand words as words. They associate certain sounds with certain commands and get to learn what they must do when they hear the sounds. Actually, I have a number of patients who do seem to understand words and whose owners have to spell out certain words that they don't want the dogs to hear.

There are some basic commands that every puppy should be taught; the most important command for the dog to understand is "No!" You have to make him know you mean it. "Quiet" should also be taught early in his life—and he should stop his noise immediately.

Training Rules—

—The best time for training the puppy is before he is fed, so that he will be looking forward to the reward of a good meal.

—For a satisfactory training program the puppy should have complete confidence in you.

—Never train a puppy while you are in a bad mood or have lost control of your emotions. Especially don't lose patience and kick a puppy in anger or throw things at him. He is still a babe in arms and cannot be expected to grasp everything at once.

—Allow only one member of the family to teach him commands and tricks. Once he has learned them all thoroughly, then others can help.

—Always talk to a dog before you approach him. This goes for any dog. Let him know you are his friend.

—Don't confuse a puppy by giving him inconsistent commands.

—Don't punish the dog with a training lead or other training object, or he will become fearful of training.

—Don't allow the training periods to get so long that the puppy becomes tired or bored.

—A puppy should never be picked up by his ears—as one of our Presidents found out, much to his chagrin.

Dos and Don'ts of Training

Dos

1. *Do* have only one, and the same, person in charge of the training program. More than one person giving commands can confuse the dog and make learning more difficult. Once the dog has learned all the commands, other members of the family can contribute to further training.

2. *Do* train the dog at the same time and place each session. Continuity and familiarity aid in the learning process.

3. *Do* be patient, kind, and gentle. The younger the dog, the easier and shorter the training sessions should be. They should be no longer than five minutes in the beginning. You can gradually increase the intensity and length (but never longer than 15-20 minutes) of the sessions as the commands are learned.

4. *Do* use the same tone of voice when giving commands. Shouting and screaming only confuse and deter learning.

5. *Do* be consistent with your commands so the dog will know what you are striving for. Use the same words and signals. Proceed with a new command only after the dog has learned previous commands.

6. *Do* use a training collar in the initial teaching of commands. As the dog learns, the learning will be reinforced with off-lead sessions.

7. *Do* reward and punish. Praise him when he follows instructions; indicate your displeasure when he doesn't. Let him know you are serious.

8. *Do* play with the dog after the training sessions as a sort of reward for his serious concentration.

Don'ts

1. *Don't* attempt to train a dog after meals or exercise. The dog will be sluggish both mentally and physically.

2. *Don't* make the training sessions long. Start with five minutes and gradually extend them to 15-20 minutes as the dog matures.

3. *Don't* expect miracles. It takes a minimum of four lessons to learn a command, and some dogs take longer.

4. *Don't* lose your patience. Shouting and screaming only confuse the dog.

5. *Don't* hit the dog in a fit of temper. If scolding is needed, be sure he understands why. Talk to him and try to explain his deficiencies.

6. *Don't* proceed with a new command until he has mastered the one you are attempting to teach. It will only confuse him.

7. *Don't* use a spiked training collar to try to impress commands on a dog. Cruelty does not help obedience training.

8. *Don't* allow playing during the sessions. Be serious. Make him realize that you mean business.

9. *Don't* reward him with a tidbit for each successful response. He'll be spoiled into expecting such a reward. Praise is enough. Tidbits can be given at the end of the training session.

10. *Never, never* let a training session end with the dog getting his own way or he will believe he can lead you. It must end only when he has followed a command and you have proven your authority and leadership.

6 COMMON QUERIES

BEHAVIOR

How can a new puppy be kept from crying all night?

Until the puppy gets used to sleeping without the warmth of his mother and litter mates, a hot-water bottle or an electric heating pad may be enough to simulate their warmth. A loud-ticking alarm clock will sometimes distract a puppy from crying. If these don't work, a baby aspirin, tranquilizer, or sleeping pill is in order until he gets used to being alone.

Is there a best way to housebreak a puppy?

Use reward and punishment, patience and perseverance, but most of all take him out at least every two hours on schedule. This should include first thing in the morning, shortly after each meal, and just before bed at night. When he errs, he should know what he has done wrong; most dogs catch on quickly. It takes anywhere from 2 weeks to 3 months, depending on the dog's age and intelligence.

Do dogs dream?

All indications are that they do. When they move their legs as if running, and whine and grunt during sleep, it is a sub-conscious expression of their thoughts. There is an old-folk superstition that to find out what a dog is dreaming you will soon know if you put a straw between his toes.

When should one begin training a puppy in the basic commands?

The best age to start training a puppy is as early as possible, but a 6- to 8-week-old puppy cannot be expected to immediately comprehend. After 3 months of age the commands will begin sinking in, and at 6 months more intensive training can be started. The discipline for a young puppy should be gentle, as he can easily be intimidated and his confidence destroyed.

Is it true that mongrels are healthier and smarter than pure-breds?

No. The veterinary hospitals are filled with as many sick mongrels as purebreds. Canines are similar to the humans who master them. There are both sickly and healthy dogs as well as dumb and smart ones in both mongrels and purebreds.

Which breed is smartest and best for training?

No breed has a monopoly on brains, and it has been proved conclusively that any breed is capable of competing in obedience-training programs and contests.

Can a show dog also be a good pet?

It is a common misconception that show dogs are too nervous to be gentle, loving pets. Many champion dogs have been house pets all their lives.

Do puppies remember their mothers, and vice versa?

The mother-puppy relationship is basically instinct. Once the puppies are weaned and leave their mother, I don't believe that mothers and offspring know one another.

Why do dogs roll on manure or dead animals?

In primitive days the dog rolled in something putrid to disguise his body scent so that when hunting, his prey would not be forewarned. No amount of scolding or discipline will stop a modern dog from doing it if this is one of his habits. Unfortunately the more putrid the odor, the more such a dog seems to enjoy rolling in it.

What are some of the primitive instincts that dogs still have?

As well as the above, the burying of bones goes back to ancestral days. Another is walking in circles before lying down to sleep. And finally, when a dog is frightened by another dog, or by any animal, he will tuck his tail between his legs, cower, and sometimes lie on his back as a sign of submission.

Can a dog grieve himself sick when left in a boarding kennel or hospital?

The average dog adjusts quickly and easily to environment, and even a shy and timid dog soon relaxes with a few kind words and a pat on the head. Even a pampered pet, with a tranquilizer, will relax enough to eat and adjust to his environment. Dogs don't grieve and die of a broken heart, nor do they forget their masters even after years of separation.

Will spaying or castration affect a dog's disposition or personality?

The dog's basic personality will not be changed by the operation. The operation doesn't make the male or female mean; if anything it makes them sweeter and more affectionate. For nervous or aggressive dogs I advise the operation because it quiets them down and prevents them from reproducing puppies with these undesirable traits.

Which makes a better house pet, a male or a female?

Pro and con can be argued indefinitely. Either sex makes the "one and only pet in your life." The female presents problems twice a year when she is in heat, and the male has the occasional urge to visit a girl friend and is not as fastidious in his habits.

Is there a right way to respond to an unfriendly dog?

Stand still, and by all means the hands should be kept still. Face him and let him evaluate your scent. Talk to him in a pleasant voice all the time he is appraising you.

Is physical punishment permissible or to be avoided?

For those dogs who insist on trying to dominate their owners, verbal punishment is often not enough. However, I advocate only mild thrashing with nothing more hurtful than a rolled-up newspaper. Overzealousness in punishment can intimidate a young dog and ruin it for life. Hitting a dog with a bare hand can cause it to become hand-shy, and yelling and kicking accomplish nothing.

Are there special ways to handle or treat an aggressive dog?

If the normal methods such as obedience training and/or a strong show of dominant ownership do not work, the battle is not lost. Other methods include tranquilizers, barbituates, electric shock treatment, pre-frontal lobotomy, and blood-letting.

Are there special ways to handle a shy, timid dog?

Tenderness and patience are the prime requisites. The dog is insecure around people and has to have its faith in the human race restored. Whether caused by an "unhappy childhood experience" or inherited, although the latter takes longer to overcome, there is hope for even the most nervous dog.

Is there a way to control tug-of-war when it gets out of hand?

It's a game to be avoided in the first place. It teaches a dog bad habits and may affect his temperament. It can also affect the formation of teeth in a young dog. If you hold the other end of something and let a dog pull on it, he may not be able to distinguish play periods from serious destruction of property and it will teach him to chew on objects around the house. Incidentally, don't give him an old shoe to chew on if you have any respect for your new shoes or those of your family.

Are there ways to keep a dog from wandering from home?

First, attempt to find out why he leaves home. It could be due to loneliness and boredom, and he might join a group of other dogs because of lack of human companionship. It could well be due to sexual frustration or lack of exercise. When the dog returns from a jaunt, don't punish him or he may not come home the next time. But also don't be over-delighted at his return. In other words, treat him with reserved feelings but show him that you still love him. If you can't find the cause, get the dog interested in obedience training. It will help both dog and owner.

When disciplining a dog does it matter where you hit it?

Only when it is being punished for biting or chewing should it be struck on the muzzle. For other forms of misdemeanor, a rolled-up newspaper applied to the hind quarters should be sufficient.

Is there some way to cure a dog from fear of thunderstorms?

Many dogs are fearful because they sense fear in their owners. I have known owners who retreat to a closet, with their dogs, to tremble together throughout a storm. One practical measure is to record a storm on a cassette, and then at intervals of a few days play it back at various volume levels until the dog is used to the sound.

Are there dog-proof wastebaskets and garbage pails?

Few dogs are free from the urge to get into wastebaskets and garbage pails—the food odors and loose papers are too enticing to be left unravaged. For correction, you need half a dozen mousetraps.

Set them, unbaited, under paper in the baskets and pails. After a few days of traps snapping and jumping at him, the trash should go unmolested.

How can dogs be kept from climbing onto chairs and sofas?

Here, too, mousetraps are a fine solution, although the family may complain a bit until programmed to watch where they sit. Set them unbaited, under papers, and the dog should soon get the point.

How can a dog be stopped from jumping on people?

There are three easy ways. The first consists of gently stepping on the hind toes while the front paws are against you. The second is to grab the front paws and rush him backward until he falls over. The third method is to bend your knee and bump him in the chest. In each case, use a stern, firm, "No!"

Is there any way to cure a dog from excessive barking?

Empty tin cans are quite effective in this regard . . . several tied together to make a good clatter. When the dog barks, throw the cans so that they land close to him (but don't hit him) and reinforce the action with a stern, "No!" If you are consistent he will soon associate barking with tin cans and your admonition will soon suffice.

Is chaining a dog a good solution for a fenceless backyard?

Not nearly so good as a fence or a pen. If there are trees around, the dog could become entangled and choke. If the dog is small it could be attacked by larger dogs in the neighborhood. Also, it is frustrating to a dog to be so confined and he could become overly aggressive.

Is obedience training important?

It almost always is in the larger breeds, and it never goes amiss in the smaller breeds. It is good for both dog and owner. The most important thing for every dog to know is that it's owner is dominant over it, as every owner should know. Professional obedience training also teaches the dog how to interact with other dogs.

Is there a magic cure for keeping a puppy from chewing everything in sight?

It's hard to apply magic to puppies, but there are several practical ways. The most practical, of course, is to keep chewable things high and dry and provide him with an ample supply of safe (India rubber and rawhide) toys. If you catch him in the act, a good deterrent is to bandage his jaws shut. Wrap the cloth lightly about his jaws, tie it under his chin, and then behind his ears. After a couple of times, he'll decide it's better not to chew.

How can a dog be broken of the car-chasing habit?

This works best with the cooperation of neighbors. Have a neighbor drive by, brake to a screeching halt, yell at the dog to startle him, and throw empty tin cans at him. One treatment will not cure the dog—it may take a dozen times—but it should finally sink in. And when it does, praise the dog as he stands quietly by while the car passes.

7 YEAR-ROUND CARE FOR COMFORT AND WELL-BEING

The house dog is the prisoner of his master, subject to his master's mode of living. The outside dog—the roamer—adapts himself, and his coat becomes thicker and longer to protect him from cold weather and snow, but the house dog is often the victim of overheating. His comfort and well-being depend on how well his master provides for his summerizing and winterizing with the change of seasons.

During their ancestral days dogs were forced to make adjustments to the climate, and they were able to withstand seasonal changes much better than today's pets. Only the hardiest dogs survived. Today's dogs have no need to race across ice packs or hot desert sands. They have lost their heavy undercoats and are physically more refined.

Since most of our pets stay indoors most of the time, in heated houses during the winter and in air-conditioned, low-humidity dwellings during the summer—contrary to what nature intended —we have to make various adjustments for them to help nature along. Today's dogs need special care with their skin, their undercoats, their haircuts. They have to be handled differently during each season. And that explains this chapter on the year-round care of the dog.

GENERAL GROOMING

Many people think that dog grooming is a mysterious art which takes a lot of time and professional training. Actually most of the tricks of a good grooming program can be learned in a short time. Because dogs enjoy the special attention they receive in grooming (along with discipline and training), regular grooming becomes established in the pet's mind and he looks forward to it. Grooming is essential to health and well-being.

Three types of hair coats have to be considered: (1) short-haired, such as Dalmatian, dachshund, and beagle, which is relatively easy to keep well groomed; (2) long-haired, such as poodle and terrier, which needs trimming often; and (3) heavy-coated or shaggy, such as old English sheep dog and Afghan hound, which requires daily combing and brushing.

The aim of all good grooming is to have a full glossy coat. It is much easier to prevent matted hair by frequent brushing than to try to restore a coat that is full of mats. Unless dogs such as the old English sheep dog and the Afghan hound are brushed and combed diligently, matted hair develops, and in extreme cases combing the mats becomes impossible and a complete clipping is necessary, much to the embarrassment of the dog. Incidentally, there are some excellent shampoos on the market which help untangle matted hair.

In many of the long-haired breeds it is recommended that the thick tufts of hair between the toes be carefully cut away, as is done with the poodle. This hair tends to ball up into felt-like mats, and it is a perfect landing place for burs, stickers, and foxtails, which is all painful and can cause lameness.

Long nails can cause foot problems. Any dog owner can become proficient in nail clipping. If you cut too deeply and the quick bleeds, use alum powder or a styptic pencil to stop the bleeding. Clip the dew claws also.

In keeping the eyes clean, a mild salt-water solution applied with cotton or soft tissue is excellent.

The dog's mouth should be checked regularly. His teeth can be cleaned with a damp cloth dipped in salt and soda. When there is tartar, the veterinarian should be called on to remove it.

For removing tar or chewing gum from a dog's hair, nail-polish remover is excellent. Don't allow the solution onto the dog's skin, and wash the hair part immediately with soap and water.

BATHING

First comb out the hair until it is free of all mats or snarls, since soap will not rinse out of them. Apply petroleum jelly or mineral oil around the eyes to keep them free from soap. Put a big wad of cotton in each ear. Fill the tub with water up to the dog's knees and thoroughly soak him. Use lukewarm water. When you and the dog are both wet, apply a mild non-irritating shampoo and work the suds in completely, starting at the head and working back. Use your fingers to work the soap down to the skin, and don't neglect the ears or paws. Use a damp washcloth to clean the face. Rinse away the suds completely; incomplete rinsing will dull the coat and irritate the skin. After the water is drained from the tub, wrap the dog in a large bath towel and wipe off the excess water before he shakes. After he has shaken himself well, you can towel him dry or use a hair dryer. Don't let him get into a draft while he is drying. On a warm sunny day he can be taken out, but don't put him in an area where he will have access to dirt or gravel, for he may roll in it.

I would generally refrain from bathing a puppy under 3 months of age. However, if odor, dirt, or parasites necessitate a bath, then it is all right to go ahead if you are careful to avoid chilling the puppy. Wrap him in a towel and hand-dry him thoroughly before letting him run around in the house. To make sure he will avoid drafts or a chilling wind, don't allow him outdoors for at least 12 hours.

SHEDDING

During the wild days the long hours of summer sunlight activated the dog into shedding his heavy winter coat. Modern-day artificial conditions have the shedding cycle confused. With thermal control, air conditioning, and electric lighting, the indoor dog doesn't know at what time of the year to grow a new coat. Therefore some dogs shed their coats around the calendar.

Normally the dog sheds his undercoat when the weather gets

hot. He gets rid of the dead hair and then grows a new coat. Cold fresh air aids nature in stimulating the circulation of the blood to the hair, which results in a glistening, shining coat.

During shedding usually the woolly undercoat comes out in rolls and chunks, and it is up to the owner to help nature along by combing out the loose hair every day. It should be removed with a wire brush or a blunt-toothed comb. Go right down to the skin with the brush or comb; the old hair will cling, causing mats, and any dead hair will cling. Undercoat left is liable to cause skin irritation. The undercoating is useful in winter but is unnecessary in summer. The long silky hair that is left keeps the dog looking beautiful and insulates him from the hot summer sun.

For short-haired dogs some people use brushes, and others use hand gloves. A vacuum cleaner is excellent for pulling out the loose hair, and so is a hacksaw blade. Dogs who live in the house year round have a tendency to skin dryness and dandruff, which is why I recommend that wheat-germ oil, vegetable oil, or bacon or fat be added to the daily diet. Normally if all the loose hair is removed daily, the average dog will shed his entire coat in a couple of weeks. The quicker the old coat is removed, the sooner there is a shiny, healthy new hair glow.

SUMMERIZING

There are many fallacies regarding the "dog days" of July and August. Dog days originated in Egypt with Sirius, the Dog Star, which is visible during a 40-day period coinciding with sultry heat. It was assumed that because during this period the dog was irritable, hung his tongue far out, slobbered and sought eagerly for scarce water, it was an evil season. It was believed that the dog was possessed by devils, that his bite was poisonous and contained the rabies germ. Even today people believe that dogs are prone to madness during dog days. Rabies, however, is not seasonal; it is a year-round disease.

Dogs require proportionally more air for breathing than humans, and since the dog perspires through his tongue he is affected by the heat more quickly. After all, he wears almost the same coat winter and summer.

Actually dogs also perspire through the pads of their feet and slightly through their skin pores. But they perspire chiefly through their tongues; consequently in hot weather the dog pants more and tends to slobber. The more he pants, the more relief he feels.

Housing

During hot weather a favorite spot for the dog is a shady corner of the yard where he can dig a deep hole and lie against the cool earth. He also enjoys the basement of the house. If he is lucky enough to live with air conditioning, he enjoys the cool, dry air as much as does his owner.

The dog's house or sleeping quarters should be in a cool and shady spot. A shaded screened-in porch is excellent. If the dog is to be outdoors, he must have a shady place.

Although puppies require a lot of fresh air, they should not be exposed long during the heat of the day, as they are susceptible to heatstroke of sunstroke. Their runs should be protected by shade trees or canvas. Aluminum roofing is excellent, as it repels the rays of the sun.

Some dogs are especially susceptible to heatstroke—the short-nosed breeds, such as pug, Boston terrier, and English bull. They must have special care. They should be kept from direct sun, in a cool place, and not overexercised in the heat of the day.

Sanitation of kennel quarters during the summer is especially important because rubbish and debris attract flies and mosquitoes, which are a constant annoyance and irritation. By keeping the area around the dog's quarters clean and by spraying and disinfecting daily, the incidence of pests can be greatly reduced.

Diet

The dog eats less during hot weather. This is nature's way of protecting him from excessive heat. Most dogs prefer to eat late in the evening, when it is cooler.

Carbohydrates and starches should be limited during hot weather. The diet may be reduced by one half to one quarter. Less body heat is required, and the dog uses less energy.

Food should not be left out, as it will easily spoil. Dishes should be washed and disinfected daily.

Unlike humans, dogs don't need extra salt in the summer. They usually get enough salt from the commercial dog foods and table scraps.

In hot weather the dog should have free access to cool, clean water at all times. Allow him to drink as much as he wants—unless he is overheated, and then he will tend to drink too much and become nauseated.

Excercise

During hot weather the dog should be taken out only when it is coolest—in early morning or late evening.

Some dogs like to wade in water or swim. This is fine exercise, and a good way to cool off. However, if there is a wind or it is a slightly chilly day, dry the dog well after each swim.

The Summer Death Trap: The Car

Invariably, every summer many dogs are brought to me either dead or just about gone from heatstroke caused by leaving them too long in a car. *On hot days a car is a very dangerous place to leave a dog.* Park the car in the shade with the windows as wide open as is consistent with the dog's not being able to jump out, and be sure to check the dog's condition frequently.

Air-conditioned cars are a great help but dangerous when the motor is stopped and the air conditioning off. Some people go off for a "few minutes," only to find the dog in distress or dead upon their return.

The early signs of heat prostration are staggering, panting, and gasping. Put ice packs on the dog's head, pull his tongue forward so it doesn't choke him, and rush him to a veterinarian. If he is in bad shape, a spot of brandy or black coffee may be given as a stimulant.

Sometimes these animals can be saved, but unfortunately there is often brain damage, and with the ensuing complications they will not survive.

Clipping

In hot weather the dog should be kept especially clean and well-groomed. He likes being cool and refreshed too.

The subject of hair clipping is much discussed. I feel that moderation is the answer. I don't approve of shaving a dog's hair down to the skin; at least half an inch of hair should be left to protect him from the sun and from fleas, ticks, and lice.

Long-haired dogs may be more comfortable in the summer if their coats are thinned out or trimmed. But never shave a dog unless it is necessary for treatment of a skin disease.

Summer Skin Ailments

During hot weather dogs are subject to many more skin conditions because fungus is more in evidence, and fleas, ticks, and lice are more plentiful.

Fleas are the greatest cause of summer eczemas. A recent survey lists the flea as the cause of over 70 percent of summer skin problems. Prophylactic measures are the best means of preventing such problems—flea collars, flea sprays and powders, and periodic baths with a flea shampoo.

About 50 percent of all dogs are acutely sensitive to flea bites, and such dogs will itch and scratch incessantly from a single bite.

If lice, fleas, or ticks are present, brush the dog over a piece of white paper and crush the varmints when they fall. A good insecticide, either spray or powder, should be applied and brushed right down to the skin. When examining for ticks, look at the ears, loins, and between the toes. Use a tweezer or thumb and finger. Gradual pressure should be applied, otherwise the head will remain embedded. If the tick has a strong hold on the skin, a drop of turpentine or nail-polish remover will shock it sufficiently to release its hold. Then the tick should be burned or crushed.

For the dog who does a lot of running in the woods and consequently picks up many ticks, a good bedding of cedar shavings is an excellent way to reduce infestation, as the odor of cedar seems to discourage most parasites.

Flies worry the dog, since they bite and cause irritation. German shepherds and chows are especially sensitive to fly bites on the tips of their ears, and many have thick, scabby lesions because of it. Fly repellants, wax or tar on the ears, and medicated ointments are all helpful.

Mosquitoes are especially dangerous to the dog because they are the intermediate hosts of heartworms. When an infected mosquito sucks on a dog's blood and then bites another dog, the second dog will have adult heartworms within a few months. In mosquito-infested areas, if possible the dog should be kept in the house at night or in screened quarters.

Summer eczema is caused by fungus and by allergies to plants, grasses, pollens, and dust. That is why grooming every day is a must in hot weather.

A skin disease often seen in hot weather is "hot spots," which is a dermatitis characterized by itching skin and red and inflamed spots which exude moisture. Recovery is slow because the dog continually mutilates his skin with his tongue or by scratching with his dirty paws. The disease is also called weeping mange, but it has no connection with mange or ringworm. It is usually caused by fungus which the dog contacts from grass; it intensifies in severity by a secondary infection. Treatment consists in covering the area wth medicated powders, surgical dressings, and ointments and lotions that are soothing and healing and destroy the fungus infection.

Some dogs are sensitive to the sun and get sunburned. White dogs are more susceptible to the sun, parasites, allergies, and skin diseases than black-haired dogs. Short-haired dogs should not be left in the sun for long. The collie is especially susceptible to sun on his face and muzzle. Suntan lotion is helpful.

Mere hot weather causes itchy skin in some dogs. It is well to keep them out of direct sun and cool. Dirty skin intensifies skin problems. In warm weather, bathing every 2 weeks should be sufficient for the average house dog. Strong flea soaps and disinfectant soaps should be avoided. Combing with a metal stripping comb, getting at the undercoat, is helpful.

The Ears and Eyes

Ear infections seem to be more prevalent during the summer months, as the hot, moist condition that develops inside the ear canal is a great place for ear mites and fungus infections. The ears and eyes should be examined daily for dust and pollen.

Clean ears with cotton swabs dipped in alcohol or peroxide. Any black material in the canal is a sign that ear mites are present; after the ear has been cleaned, an ear-mite preparation should be inserted. Examine for ticks, as the ear is a favorite hiding place.

Summer Colds

Summer colds occur because warm days with chilly nights affect susceptible pets. A slight chill often leads to colds, tonsillitis, bronchitis, and other respiratory infections.

A word of caution regarding summer chill in puppies: Puppies can be playing happily in the sunshine one minute and almost immediately, with the disappearance of the sun, be shivering in a chilly wind. This is dangerous for the puppy; there easily develops a cold or more severe infection, such as pneumonia or distemper.

Spring is often dangerous because of the changeable weather. When putting out young dogs or toy breeds, see that they don't get cold, or provide a shelter into which they can retire if the weather should change.

Dry Nose

A dry nose during the hot summer is not necessarily a sign that the dog has a temperature. Such weather will usually keep the nose in a hot, dry condition but in fine health. Don't become concerned unless fever and lassitude are present.

Additional Summer Tips

When walking a dog on hot days, be wary of asphalt or tar. Either will cause a painful condition in the dog's pads. To remove such material from the pads, rub with pure lard or salad oil. Don't use turpentine or kerosene; these are irritating and can cause infected feet.

Many dogs are afraid of thunder and lightning and have hysterics during storms. Some actually go out of their heads. Many just need petting and to be with their owners. For others, heavy tranquilization and sedation is needed to calm them down.

It is amazing how most dogs can foretell summer storms long before they hit. Scientists believe that the dog's hearing is so acute that he can hear the high winds approaching miles away. ESP researchers believe that dogs can foretell approaching storms because of the sixth sense they possess.

Shipping a Dog in Summer

During the hot summer months the dog should travel mostly at night or early in the morning. This can be arranged with the airline or express company. Don't ship the dog on weekends or over holidays; he might have to stay in the crate several extra days. The crate should be wire or else with a lot of open ventilation. The person on the receiving end should meet the dog and get him out of the crate promptly. The dog should then be given some cool water and a light meal and allowed to rest. Most airlines and express companies take special care of animals.

WINTERIZING

During the winter months, when sickness and disease are especially prevalent, the dog's health should be under constant surveillance. His health is dependent on housing, diet, exercise, and general treatment.

By keeping the dog healthy his natural resistance to disease-producing germs is increased. Annual booster vaccination of D-H-L each fall is especially recommended. Probably two of the most neglected predisposing sources of infection are bad ventilation and unsatisfactory sanitation in the kennel or living quarters.

Housing

Indoor Dogs. In primitive days dogs had thick coats and rugged bodies. With heated houses, their coats don't have to be so thick and they need the protection of a coat or sweater when they go outside into cold temperatures. Even heavy-coated dogs should wear a blanket when left in a car for long periods of time in cold weather.

The toy breeds and small pets need the warmth and dryness of our houses because of their rearing and their dependence on us to provide them with warmth. Be sure to keep a dog's bed away from radiators, as the heat is drying to the coat.

Most of our pets sleep indoors, sometimes under sheets and blankets. Some pets even sleep on their backs with their feet in the air, mimicking their masters, complete with such sound effects as snoring.

Outdoor Dogs. For the indoor dog a good temperature to maintain is about 65 degrees. For the outdoor dog, if the temperature goes down into the 20's or even below zero, so long as he is protected from the wind and drafts and has good bedding, he will stay warm and snug. Few breeds of outdoor dogs need their living quarters heated.

The most important thing is dry, draftless sleeping quarters. In other words, if the dog sleeps outdoors he should have a dry, well-insulated house protected from wind. It should not face the cold north. In severe cold an empty burlap sack or curtain should be nailed over the opening of his house, and he will soon learn to walk under it. If there is more than one dog, usually they will sleep curled up together for warmth. Where the weather is severe, if the dog is old or a nursing bitch, infrared bulbs or regular electric bulbs are recommended for added heat.

There are many refined types of houses, but a simple box that is waterproof can be suitable living quarters for the outdoor dog. If possible, put the house against a protecting wall and certainly away from the north winds.

If possible, keep the dog's bed at least 4 inches off the floor. Use good bedding, at least 5 inches thick, for the dog to curl up in. Old blankets, old rugs, or cedar or pine shavings are best.

Diet

During the cold winter months there should be an increase in starches and carbohydrates to provide more heat and energy. Nourishing foods, warm foods, and extra vitamin supplements are advisable. I recommend increasing by one quarter the amount of food in the winter months. The dog should not be allowed to drink freezing water; it will chill his tummy and upset his bowels. Water should be at room temperature.

Exercise

In winter weather, no matter how cold or damp, there should be daily exercise. When a house pet is outside, so long as he is active let him stay, but he should not be allowed to sit around or lie on the cold ground or in the snow for any length of time, else he will get chilled. He will then be susceptible to tonsillitis, pneumonia, or other disease.

When there is snow, it is safer to walk a dog on a leash. Dogs have a natural tendency to walk in the ploughed areas and dart across the road heedless of cars. Most dogs love to wade in snowdrifts, and it is amusing to watch a puppy in his first snow. The minute he gets inside, dry him to keep him from chilling. Outdoor dogs love to be outside all the time, and the colder it gets the more they seem to enjoy it, but the indoor dog should not be allowed outdoors for long periods.

After he has been out in snow and ice, special attention should be paid to the dog's feet. Ice and snowballs develop in the webbing between the toes. If the dog has come in contact with sanded walks, the defrosting agents can be irritating to his sensitive pads. The chemicals should be washed from the feet immediately. If allowed to remain, they can cause severe irritation, and should the dog lick his pads the chemicals can irritate his tongue.

Health Check

All dogs should be routinely checked twice a year: before cold weather and before hot weather—a 1,000 mile checkup! Also, all dogs should be given an annual booster shot of D-H-L in the fall of the year to fully protect them during the dangerous winter months.

Young animals and older ones should be given extra consideration. In the older ones, if they have arthritis or rheumatism, the cold weather increase the pain, and extended exposure to cold increases the suffering.

Bathing

Baths should be given less often during cold weather. An outdoor dog should not need bathing at all during the winter months except under emergency conditions. How often to bathe your dog is up to you, and if he sleeps with you or is in your lap most of the time, you probably will want to bathe him more often. But don't take him outdoors for at least 3 to 4 hours after bathing, when he is thoroughly dry.

Brushing, sponging, and dry shampooing at weekly intervals are usually sufficient for the average indoor dog, bathing him only when necessary. Corn meal or corn starch does a good job in short- or medium-haired breeds. For white dogs corn starch brushed in removes the dust and dirt and leaves the dog as white as a snowball.

Both young and old dogs are susceptible to chilling after a bath, and any dampness of the coat will render them prone to tonsillitis, bronchitis, and distemper.

TRAVELING BY CAR

As mentioned earlier, during the summer months always park the car in the shade with the windows open as far as possible, because the car can quickly become an oven.

When traveling with a dog during summer, a thermos jug of crushed ice and water should be readily available. I also advise wetting several towels with cold water and putting them on the floor for the dog to lie on.

Before going on a long trip, visit your veterinarian for a health certificate (in some states, and in Mexico and Canada, this is required) and get a rabies booster shot if he is due for one.

For a dog who is excitable, a wire cage is a good idea because then the windows can be lowered sufficiently to give him ample air circulation while you are parked or away from the car.

Don't leash a dog to the window, or tie him up inside the car, as he might easily hang himself.

Don't feed the dog much before you start or on the trip. It is wise to carry a supply of water in a thermos. Stop every few hours to exercise the dog—the roadside parks are becoming popular for both humans and animals.

Most dogs curl up and sleep during a long car ride. However, there are some excitable animals who need sedation, and your veterinarian can prescribe tranquilizers that will keep your dog quiet and prevent drooling or vomiting. Sedatives or tranquilizers with anti-nausea qualities seem to give better results than dramamine or bonamine, which don't seem to work as well on dogs as on humans.

INDEX

hysterectomies, 45, 50
hysteria, 49

immunizations, shots for, 65
impotence, 46
infantile autism in dogs, 84
inner-ear infections, 38
instincts, 22-28
intelligence in dogs, 10-15
intestinal parasites, *see* worms
introversion, 50
Irish wolfhounds, 21

jackals, 9
jealousy in dogs, 42, 45

kennels, 80, 91
  boarding, 64
kennelitis, 84
Kerry blue terriers, 11, 91
kidneys, diseases of, 40, 60
  see also nephritis

leash, use of, 82, 83
  in puppy training, 70, 71
lice, 80, 101
long-coated breeds, grooming, 96

male dogs, as house pets, 91
manure, rolling in, 91
mass hysteria, 49
masturbation, 51
maternal instinct, 23-24, 25
milk fever, *see* eclampsia
mineral deficiency, *see* vitamins and
  minerals, deficiencies
minerals, *see* vitamins and minerals
miscarriages, 46
mosquitoes as heartworm carriers,
  102
muzzling, 53, 58, 59

nails, clipping, 61, 101
names, teaching puppy, 85
narcotics, *see* tranquilizers
nephritis, 40
nervousness, inherited, 37-38
neuro-dermatitis, 49
neuroses, 37, 41, 47, 57, 59, 60
  treatment of, 63

see also psychosomatic ailments
normal behavior, 30
nursing puppies, 19
  see also puppies

obedience-training classes, 29, 48,
  58, 62
organic problems, as cause of
  abnormal behavior, 38-39
overdependency, 62
overfeeding, danger of, 41
  for puppies, 66, 74, 76-77, 82
owner's responsibility for dogs, 55

paper training, 69-70
parasites, 65, 80
  see also worms
pedigreed dogs, 9
Pekingese, 43
personality, 17
  types, 9
  as factor in training, 31
pet shops, 80
phobias, 50
pointers, 21
poisoning symptoms and treatment,
  38
poodles, 9, 22, 91, 96
predicting storms, 12
prenatal influences, 18-19
prevention of accidents in
  housebreaking, 68
primitive instincts, 91
problem dogs, handling, 37, 39, 41
  63
prostate gland, 40
prostatitis, 60
protective instinct, 59
protein, necessity for, in puppy
  feeding, 71-72
pseudohermaphrodites, 51
psi-trailing, 13-15
psychosomatic ailments, 41-47
  see also neuroses
pug dogs, 43, 99
punishment, 33, 52, 58, 61
puppies, "demand feeding," 74
  teething, 75, 77-78
  hand raising, 24-25
  crying, 89